MY LIFE AS A LEMON

[F. M. Ellis]

Copyright © 2020 **F. M. Ellis**

All rights reserved.

All rights reserved. No part of this book may be reproduced in any form by an electronic or mechanical means, including information storage and retrieval systems, without permission in writing from the publisher, except by a reviewer who may quote brief passages in a review.

This Is for Those Who Find Themselves Wandering.

You Are on The Right Track…Enjoy!

The vibration startled me as I began to wake. My body was slightly jolted as the 18 wheeler drove by seemingly at speeds faster than the law allowed. As my eyes slowly opened, I sat in a daze trying to make sense of my view. My heart skipped a few beats, and my chest tightened as I realized I had done it again. A night full of partying and heavy drinking had me hungover but alive. I briefly pondered on how many of my nine lives I had used. I was parked on the shoulder of Interstate 285 outside Atlanta. I could see the wind gently relocating leaves from one part of the highway to another. I looked around my vehicle in a daze for clues. Something to explain what the hell happened. I took inventory of my possessions, and the strong smell of vomit caught my attention. Thank goodness God watches over babies and fools. Since I was in my thirties, I fell into the latter of the two categories. From a distance, I looked like a young woman who had pulled off the road to take a call or look up directions. But upon further observation, one could see the dark circles under my eyes or the dried vomit on my face. I was lucky to be alive and slightly terrified that maybe someone else, at my expense, was not. I had no recollection of how I ended up in my car and asleep on the side of the interstate.

The orange light on the dashboard indicated that I needed to get gas. Strangely, I started the night out with a full tank. I slowly exited the passenger side to see if there was any damage from a possible collision. Nope. It was still shiny and clean from the car wash the day before. I got back in the car, almost passing out from my abrupt movements, and just sat there for a minute. I looked at my surroundings again; people were racing to church, grocery shopping, or leaving a lover's house from the night before. The things regular people were doing on a Sunday morning. But not me. I was sitting on the side of a busy interstate, trying to remember how I got there. This may seem crazy to the masses, but it was just another day for Fatous Ellison.

Some people have alarm clocks to wake them up. On this Sunday morning, 285-traffic was my alarm. I gathered myself and then got my ass off the highway before law enforcement stopped to check on me. Based on my location, I assumed that I had gotten on the road, headed opposite my house, pulled over to throw up, and then passed out. I was about forty minutes from home, and my head was spinning. How did I end up in the car alone? Why was I allowed behind the wheel? Who was looking for me? The questions kept coming, but the answers never did. When I pulled in front of my place an hour later, I found the courage to look at my phone. I missed a million calls but was not in the mood to talk. I showered, drank a pool full of water, fought the urge to throw up again, slowly lay on my bed, and passed out. The average person would learn from this and vow never to let it happen again. As you will learn, I am not average.

Table of Contents

IT IS WHAT IT IS 7
SONNY & MADELINE 10
WHAT KIND OF NAME IS FATOU? 15
THE THING THAT CHANGED EVERYTHING ELSE 19
FAMILY TIES 22
PLANS 27
WHERE IS SHE?! 30
BROTHERS 34
MORE PLANS 36
AND SO, IT BEGINS 39
BOYZ TO MEN 43
SPECIAL DELIVERIES 61
NAÏVE OR STUPID 68
THE GIRLS 83
ON THE EDGE 88
FAST AND EASY 92
BORN THIS WAY? 109
DOING THE MOST 112
LEFT, RIGHT, LEFT 118
FREE. NOT FREE 127
MY NEW LOVE 134
I NEED A MINUTE 142
FEELING EXHILARATED 146

SELF PROCLAIMED THREE-TIME LOSER 149
LOST AND FOUND 179
MORE OF THE SAME 184
IF IT ISN'T LOVE 189
BABY GIRL 192
THE EMPTY NEST IS UNDERRATED 197
THE MAN 199
MOVING DIFFERENTLY 217
A LETTER TO MY FAMILY 227
ABOUT THE AUTHOR 228

IT IS WHAT IT IS

Maslow's hierarchy of needs pyramid suggests that until a person has the basics taken care of, like food, clothing, and shelter, the motivation to fulfill other needs like intimate relationships, personal achievements, and living your best life is quite difficult. In my life, my family provided me with the first tiers of his pyramid with ease. After that, however, it is all about choices to grow and prosper, which involves the remaining pyramid tiers. Throughout my life, I have made some good and some unsavory choices in pursuit of self-actualization. However, the things I have seen, felt, heard, and learned along the way made me reconsider where I wanted to land on this hierarchy of needs.

Our family on Ferguson Avenue was a close-knit one, well-rounded and full of energy. We took road trips, family vacations, went to breakfast a couple of Saturday mornings a month, went for long drives, parked across from the airport, and watched the planes take off; we bowled, played putt put, rode horses, went on fishing expeditions, and had great birthday parties. I also had a close extended family, cousins, aunts, uncles, and friends. My family has seen me grow up and vice versa. I will say without a shadow of a doubt that this circle has gotten me up to the relationship part of the needs pyramid, for I learned how to interact, share, participate, lead, problem solve, show compassion, dream, how to be a mother, and run a household. They gave me a sense of pride and showed me how to stand up for myself and others and feel a part of something greater than myself. I am infinitely grateful for this. On the flip side, this is the same circle that aided me in becoming an alcoholic, promiscuous and needy. I grew up enjoying my family and friends while simultaneously wanting to distance myself from them. I felt loved but stuck. I felt included but different.

As a child, I spent considerable time at my grandmother's house. My cousin Dawn lived there with her mom, Auntie Helen, and my Uncle Holden. My parents would drop me off before dawn and pick me up after work when it was time to enter school; enrolling me at Big Hamilton, around the corner from Madear, made sense. Dawn attended this school as well, but she was leaving for a higher grade the same year I started.

When my parents purchased their own home in University City, a suburb of St. Louis, they transferred me to Pershing Elementary. Pershing provided me with a series of "firsts"—my first crush, my first real fight, and my first bout with public humiliation. My friends and I were sitting on the railing surrounding this five-foot drop covering the lower-level windows. A kickball game was going on, so we watched it from our slightly unsafe positions. I was struck in the forehead with a kickball in the middle of a hearty laugh. Wham! And I was sent over the railing, legs in the air, skirt around my neck and out of place, and my eyes as big as the area I was falling into. After bouncing on the concrete floor, I lay there, trying to gain composure. A million sets of eyes glared down at me. As far as I could see, kids were lined up and crowded around the railing in disbelief. Some were attempting to jump down and help, others were giggling and pointing, while others walked away unamused. To make it worst, I was taken to the nurses' office, which made me late for my next class.

Upon arrival to class, my teacher demanded that I write "I will not be late to class" 500 times and turn it in before I left class.

Next..." the first fight." Here is where I had my first highly anticipated three o'clock fight. My opponent was Kary Zoe. Kary had given me her money at school the day before to pick up some candy for our next field trip. Our school was going to the St. Louis Symphony. During our bus assignments, Kary and I got separated. We passed messages through other students discussing how we would meet back up to divide the candy. Unfortunately, this never happened, and Kary swore I had taken her money and candy. We rode different buses, and by the time we got back to school, Kary had told everyone she would beat my ass.

This was the fourth grade, and I had not had a smackdown for a couple of years. I felt unprepared and nervous. When the school bell rang, I started across the school lawn and headed home; a voice startled me from behind, and I knew there was no escaping. I just turned around and waited for the mob to catch up. Once they did, Kary was so kind as to explain why she would kick my butt. I listened and just waited for it to start. My heart was pounding harder than someone who had just done too much cocaine. It was too late to defuse the situation; as soon as someone from the crowd yelled, "Hit her!" Kary pushed me, and it was on. I won that fight because neither Kary nor her cheerleaders brought "the fight" up again. Everyone goes silent when the underdog wins.

SONNY & MADELINE

My mom was one of seven kids born to Octavia and Preston Armstead. She was the youngest of two sisters and sweet as pie. Some people are just born kind and caring. Madeline Ellison is that person. She met my dad whom at the time, was a DJ at a local club. They were introduced through one of my dad's cousins. My mom was a good girl, loved to dance, was very pretty, and was active in school organizations. She was homecoming runner-up in her senior year and had an easy yet wet-behind-the-ear persona. My dad was a man's man. He had little respect for the "white man's law" but abided by it. He served his country in Vietnam and got his certification in mechanical engineering. He stood about six feet two inches, stayed in shape through karate, read many books, and always put his family first.

Growing up, my parents went through some interesting stages in their attempts to find themselves or become better people. For my dad, it was black power; for my mom, it was the road to redemption. My brothers and I were caught in the crossfires of Jesus and the honorable Elijah Mohammed. Their intentions were good, but it became a tug-of-war between church and race. My dad was black power, black pride. I mean not an extremist, but very well-aware and informed. He was not a lifer, so he never chose to convert. He loved the Lord just as much as my mom but wanted to see African Americans become more financially stable and empowered by working together. I do not believe dad wanted to be classified by his religion, but he felt connected to the message of both the Honorable Elijah Mohammed and Minister Louis A. Farrakhan.

Dad would purchase our tickets to his events whenever the minister was in town. I could see the excitement and confidence that radiated from him. Hundreds of black people gathered for a great cause, greeting each other with hugs and addressing each other with terms of endearment like "my brother" or "my sister." It felt good to be part of something that celebrated me. The majority believed Farrakhan preached hate, but the hate he spoke of, was to hate what the majority thought of us and to rally together to uplift ourselves and our communities. He preached self-empowerment as opposed to waiting for a handout. Honestly, you would think people would appreciate a speech like that since some "other" groups believed we could not do shit on our own and were tired of being our saving grace.

This upbringing gave me strength, confidence, and resilience that showed up when needed. I never felt inferior to others, regardless of race or income. This thinking would be both a curse and a blessing in the upcoming years.

To accompany our ethnic growth, my dad also introduced us to Kwanzaa (an African celebration of the harvest observed during the week between Christmas Day and New Year's Day). We started going to the local YMCA to ring in the New Year as a family, Kwanzaa style. There were professional dancers in their festive African attire, music, food, games, books, you name it. For a kid, Kwanzaa was cool. There was something to entertain everyone. My parents could have chosen to watch Dick Clark bring in the New Year in Times Square or go out with their friends; instead, they invested in themselves and their children through a celebration that brought us joy while educating us. As a family, we started to consider the last night of Kwanzaa as part of our new family tradition. What a great time to be a kid.

The drawback was that most of these things were not looked upon in a favorable manner in our community. People wanted to say they were black and proud, seemingly only when some cool rapper made it part of his lyrics. The education we got at 1140 would not be so openly shared with our friends because of ignorant backlash.

My mom supported my dad's black self-awareness efforts, but she got a little carried away at the time. I remember her sewing dashikis for my brothers and me to wear to school. She even went as far as braiding my hair in the ugliest pattern ever. The day she braided my hair and laid out that hideous dashiki for me to wear was the day our trivial mother-daughter conflict started. I already have an African name, and she wanted me to walk out the house with a freaking coat of many colors and my hair braided like I just completed a 12-month prison bid? Was she crazy? Do you know how cruel kids in the sixth grade are? I wore a hat on the bus and went straight to the bathroom once I got to school. I spent the entire first period taking those stupid braids down and stuffing the dashiki in my bookbag. Black pride was one thing, but survival and self-preservation were another, and at that moment, the latter proved more important. I will say it loud, "I'm black, and I'm proud!" but I was not going to dress like I was headed to Zimbabwe to prove it. Not a chance. Come to think of it, that was my dad's movement, not mine. So, I was confused that my mom was acting like Winnie Mandela about every damn thing. This goes to show you just how my mom committed herself to something. But at times to the detriment of others. Kudos to you, Mom.

As committed as the matriarch of our family was to the black movement, she was more committed to her Lord and savior. See, the movement was all dad's arena, but the church was all moms. Mostly, I enjoyed going to church because I did not want to go to hell. That is how the church and God were presented to us, leaving people with those two choices ... go to church or go to hell. As a child, mom's church seemed forced, whereas dad's movement did not. Even the most passionate person needs a break from their passion. The church was no different.

Before I start, please understand my unhappiness with the church as a place of worship has nothing to do with my belief in a higher power. I said I felt it unnecessary for it to become an obsession. From the time I could understand words, I was in church, attending prayer meetings, choir rehearsal, and around my mom's sphere that spoke of almost nothing but church and scriptures. On the outside, people may say religion is a great foundation for a child. I somewhat agree, but life is about balance, and when it came to Jesus...we had none. Church, God, and religion were the topic of many debates between my mom and me. I was confused about how people, in general, could love someone or something they have no evidence of, yet kill rape, and outright display hatred for the people they encounter daily. The hypocrisy of it all was too much to comprehend. I challenged how the people in the black communities I saw depended on the Holy Ghost to move mountains for them while they sat on their asses doing nothing more than preaching to others about the afterlife. I saw people losing their homes and vehicles, waiting for a blessing. Those blessings typically came from someone who spent less time praying and more time planning.

My argument also addressed health and fitness. Praying and eliminating stress in your life was one thing, but minimum physical activity and bad eating habits could have one walking "the street paved in gold" sooner than necessary. Our household was active and healthy, but I cannot say the same about my other "brothers and sisters in Christ." Over the years, my relationship with God did deepen, but so did my facetiousness. But with her unwavering faith and determination, my mom was hell-bent on making sure her children went to heaven. No, it is not the worst thing a parent can want for a child; I just thought it should not be the only thing. My mother's interest extended far beyond church services, but she never pursued it back then. The woman is talented; she sketches, writes poetry, creates music, and designs clothes. Deep down, I think most of my resentment for the church came because it kept my mom from living her best life and pursuing her dreams. She seemed so consumed with where she would go after death that she forgot to live.

WHAT KIND OF NAME IS FATOU?

Fatou-Mata Ellison means beloved by all. It originates from the African continent and is used in more than one country. My parents did their best to help us identify with our heritage and African roots. The meaning of my name is special to me. Although I was not fond of the name, the meaning provided a sense of pride whenever I had the privilege to disclose it. My parents could have named me anything else; instead, they chose to set me apart from the crowd. But being unique came at a price. I got teased a lot about my name. The first day of school was always the worst. During roll call, teachers would butcher my name. I guessed the pronunciation and "sounding it out" skills they taught us did not apply to them. I could always tell when they got to me. There would be a pause, a quiet failed attempt, and finally, "the last name Ellison!" to save face. I would shake my head and reply, "It's Faye Two." When this happened, the class would laugh and start with their version of pronunciations. Everything from "Faye Three and Faye Four" to "Faye Squared," "Faye to the Second Power," and so on. No worries, teasing gave me a tough outer layer and a great sense of humor.

I often wondered how well my brothers fared with their somewhat unique names. I am sure they were teased as well. That is what kids do when something or someone is different; they tease, bully or isolate. I recall one conversation I overheard my brothers having with my mom. They claimed they legally changed their first names from Kei and Kame to Michael and Kevin. This was hilarious because they were still in elementary but serious as a heart attack. They went as far as to demand that we call them by these new names. I chuckled under my breath, knowing damn well neither one of us would address them as such, especially in front of our dad. This protest sprang from a classmate that commented that Kei had a "girl's" name. I laughed, thinking it sounded like a girl's name and that maybe I should have been called Kei instead of Fatou. I always thought his entire name was beautiful. I could see how kids got it confused. Years later, unisex names became quite common, and the "you got a girl's name!" teasing ceased.

Besides the unique names, we had a pretty good childhood. We enjoyed birthday celebrations, decorated for Christmas, took candy cards to school on Valentine's, dyed eggs for Easter, and dressed up for Halloween. Just kids being kids. Life was simple. My biggest challenges were wearing a bang to cover up my forehead, getting on my cousins Dawn's good side, and being able to stay outside later. That all changed in the summer of '79. That year symbolized my biting of the forbidden fruit. After '79, my eyes would forever be open to the things I once never knew existed. I learned shame, anger, and a coping mechanism that would not always serve me in years to come.

In 1979, my nose and trust in people were broken; what a summer. Most recently, I discovered the nose incident made me feel unimportant. It happened in my dad's hometown of Poplar Bluff, MO; this is where I spent a lot of summers with Grandma Ellison and a host of cousins. My parents would pack me up, provide me with adequate snacks, and sit me in the seat behind the Greyhound bus driver. As a child, this was the coolest way to travel. On my own, I did not have to share my snacks; and I had money in my pocket. Popular Bluff, MO, was a kids' paradise. Carefree, miles of open countryside, late nights running back and forth from Grandma Ellison's house to Aunt Eunice's. They lived directly across the road from each other. The doors were always unlocked, and there was no church on Sunday. This was my description of paradise for a kid in the seventies. Being in the backwoods of Missouri with minimum time constraints and no responsibilities, catching lightning bugs, riding in the back of pick-up trucks, fishing, and eating watermelon where shoes were optional, and so was being courteous.

One summer, my granny, cousins, and I attended a gathering in the park. We ate, played games, and told stories. At some point, a race ensued, and my cousin Lydia and I were in a dead heat to the finish. The distance could not have been more than 100 feet, but the remnants of this race would go much farther. My cousin Lydia and I were so focused on the finish line that we started to close in on each other's path. We were so close our feet got tangled, and down we both went. Lydia rolled on her side numerous times and came to a crashing stop while I went diving face-first into the hard dirt. Or shall I say nose first? I remember crying like a hungry baby. I was not sure if it was the impact or the embarrassment of a public accident that hurt the most. After my granny came to retrieve my dusty skinny body, I knew… it was the fall. We did not leave the park to seek medical attention, but we should have. If so, the injuries to my face may have been reduced if someone had taken it seriously enough. But nope, a disfigured nose was just in the cards for me after that day. My family hung out for what seemed like hours after the fall, and I guess my swollen nose and bluish bruises under my eyes were not severe enough. When we got home, my granny had thought enough of me to place an ice pack of frozen vegetables on my face to reduce the swelling. Before the fall, I had never experienced a headache, but at that moment, my head felt like a marching band was performing in the back of my eyes. I could not wait to take a bath and lie down. I am no doctor, but I believe my situation warranted a doctor's visit, if not the emergency room. Not in my case, I would have to live with my swollen, disfigured nose until I finally went to an ENT for sinus issues 17 years later.

One of my biggest problems with how that was handled is, ultimate, it was not handled at all. I interpreted it to mean I was not worth the fuss. Even when I got home, I do not recall my parents saying a word about my nose. I became annoyed, then angry. Did they not see me? I started looking in the mirror more often and needing validation about my appearance. What I developed was a sense of self. I became aware of how other girls my age looked and how each was treated. Did prettier people get more love, attention, and empathy?

THE THING THAT CHANGED EVERYTHING ELSE

It was my seventh birthday; my cousin Lydia had run a bath with powdered detergent for suds since we were out of bubble bath. My granny caught us just before we sat our naked behinds in the water. "What the hell, y'all going get your skin eaten off!". You cannot get in that water! Get your house robes on and wait 'til I get back with some bubble bath." And she was out the door. When my granny left, our older cousin Daryl came over and asked us if we wanted to play a game. Of course, we did! We were kids. The game was sort of like cops and robbers. Daryl would chase us individually through the tiny house, and he would catch us and handcuff us. It sounds like fun, right? We took turns getting arrested, and on my third time, I was handcuffed and bent over the bed. Daryl said he would be right back. To my recollection, he was gone for a while. His tardiness gave me my first encounter with intuition. I felt something was weird but was too young to understand what. Just as I started to get up from the bed, Daryl appeared and started with the rehearsed police routine. Except for this time, there were fewer words, and he seemed distracted. He demanded that I stay turned away from him, and before I knew what was happening, he lifted my robe and inserted his penis between my buttocks. It was this selfish act of betrayal that changed my trajectory. It was as if a light had been turned on where there was once necessary darkness (naivety) to protect the innocent until it was time to learn of such human behavior. This light came with suspicion of people, inability to fully trust, and countless missed love connections. To overcome the ordeal, I developed a safe place to escape to, which to my detriment, would keep me from exposing Daryl and others like him, leaving him free to roam, prey, and repeat his behavior. I was a coward. I was ill-prepared to handle situations like that, and I took the road most traveled... silence. It seemed like it would all go away if left unaddressed, but nothing could have been further from the truth. It would be revealed years later that Daryl had continued his sickening behavior and violated another relative. To his victory, she, too, chose silence. When my grandmother returned home, I bathed and prepared for my party as if nothing had happened. Life is crazy like that sometimes; one minute, you play cops and robbers with your cousins, and the next, you are being molested by one of them. That day was the first time I allowed myself to be disrespected, and by choosing to say nothing, it would not be the last time.

The events the following day would become a pattern repeated after every trauma I faced going forward. Instead of making sure the wrongdoer was punished or corrected, I would do something that put me in a compromising and downright dangerous situation. The following afternoon, Grandma, Daryl, and I went to the grocery store in her pick-up truck. I sat in the back of the pick-up, still struggling with the events of the day before. Not only had Daryl stolen my sexual innocence, but he had also put a blemish on the summers I looked forward to each year with my grandma and cousins. I wanted to keep my distance from everyone without giving away that something was wrong. I asked my granny if I could stay outside in the truck while she and Daryl went grocery shopping. To my relief, she didn't push back or force me to come. As I sat there alone with my thoughts, baking in the August sun like cookie dough, the shame and confusion I felt over the last 24 hours gave way to rage.

The longer I sat, the harder it became to control. I needed to express myself, but I did not know how. My cousin had left his shotgun sitting in the back of the pick-up, to my delight and detriment. I do not know why, but my attention was drawn to a white male resting in the back of another pick-up about 20 feet away from me. The voice in my head was louder and more aggressive than the day before. "Shoot his ass!" "Who cares anyway?" "Hurt him!". I crawled to where the shotgun rested and grabbed it like it was the last piece of candy in a Halloween dish. I felt so calm and close to it I wanted to kiss it.

Then the world went silent ... again. No birds, no kids playing, no horns honking, just me, the gun, and the voice. I can't remember if I checked the magazine or not. I cocked the gun (like I saw in the movies), placed one hand under the barrel, the other hand between the receiver and stock, then held the butt of the gun in place with my shoulder. It took a little longer than in the movies to line the barrel up with my victim, and as soon as I got him in my line of fire, I heard a different voice. This time it was panic in the distance and calling my name. I wanted to resist acknowledging it because I knew what it was saying. I slowly turned towards the store, seeing Daryl and my granny waving their hands, jumping up and down, and sprinting toward the front door. I immediately dropped the gun and sat straight up in the truck. Other than the time my dad thought Kei had gotten hit by a car, I had never seen fear like the fear in my granny's eyes when she finally reached me. Speechless, Daryl took the gun and stayed in the back, and I was instructed to sit in the front. No words were spoken. I did not cry, scream, or even react; I was frozen by what I almost did. Because even if I had missed, shit would have gotten unbelievably real for the Ellison family. The silence on the ride home spoke volumes. No in-depth conversation about the "why" and the "what if" of my actions. No punishment, no parents notified, never mentioned again. In hindsight, this was one of my first doses of getting away with murder; this was the second horrifying thing of that summer. For it allowed me to attempt the unthinkable with no consequences.

FAMILY TIES

That same fall, my parents got married. This was one of that year's highs, and it was a magical event. My mom's color of choice was baby blue. The dress, the tux, the groomsmen, me (the flower girl), and the decorations were all blue. My mom was seven months pregnant with my brother Kei, and although she was big as a house (sorry, Mom), she was truly a stunning bride. My parents were married at my mom's parents' home. It was the house my mom and her siblings grew up in, and the house my two first cousins and I considered a home away from home. I had a big curly afro, my dad had full sideburns, and my mom wore short hair with tapered curls.

Madea's house was a beautiful four-sided brick two-story on a full basement. Madea's place was usually quiet, with the daily routine of keeping her grandkids from sliding down the second-floor steps or the sounds of *The Guiding Light, As the World Turns,* or *Days of Our Lives* coming from the television. Madear could be found with her arms and ankles crossed, nodding off in her comfy chair, the radiator clicking on and off in the background. On this evening, things were all but routine. I had seen many people hanging out at Madea's house during holidays, birthdays, or prayer meetings (she occasionally hosted). But this evening was like no other. The house was packed with aunts and uncles, cousins, friends, family, neighbors, coworkers, and old classmates from both my mom's and dad's sides. My mom was glorious in her tailor-made dress. I remember how I beamed with pride as she made her grand entrance down the staircase into the living room, where she and my dad would be pronounced husband and wife. Chairs were neatly lined in rows, filling the dining and living room. Despite the efforts to accommodate as many guests as possible, there was standing room only.

The wedding would do very little to change my life. I always had both of my parents in the same home. The wedding was just to make it official and legal. I was content before they married and afterward. The day came and went without incident. Happy ever after can prove difficult with two people who started a family out of wedlock and "shacked up," to the dismay of my maternal grandparents. I did not know until much later that there was a little tension between my grandparents and my mom (for leaving her father's home unmarried to live with my father). I could see how that went against her strict Baptist upbringing.

To provide perspective on my maternal grandparents, Preston, and Octavia Armstead. My grandfather was a Mason, and Madear was an "Eastern Star." Just in case you are wondering what a Mason and Eastern Star are, let me elaborate. Simply put, Masons are the world's oldest and largest fraternity. Its membership is a who's who of world history, from George Washington to Henry Ford, Preston Armstead, and, more recently, my brother Kei. I remember very little about my mom's dad except his skin was dark and smooth as velvet, and he blessed me with his forehead. Unfortunately, pawpaw passed away from a brain aneurysm when I was four. I will forever be remembered for commenting at his funeral that I would miss him, but not his spankings. An Eastern Star is also a fraternity for both men and women. Eastern Star is a social order comprised of persons with spiritual values, but it is not a religion. Madear, or more formally Octavia, was the matriarch of the family. Through prayer and Benson and Hedges cigarettes, Madear was as strong as they came. Beautiful with pale skin that gave clues to the broken African bloodline, violated by a European male somewhere along the way. Her long black hair was sprinkled with grey highlights that she kept in a ponytail pulled to the back or a long braid going in the same direction. Her pretty heart-shaped faced was played down by the black-rimmed glasses she wore. The heavy voice of a lifelong smoker did not match the soft features God blessed her with. I would enjoy many great years and memories with Madear. She was the voice of reason and relied heavily on scripture to answer most of life's questions. She was kind of a quiet spirit with an almost standoffish demeanor until she felt comfortable with you.

Now, Ellison, on the other hand, was something different. I only saw my dad's father once. It was an informal meeting almost by accident. He was standing outside a store or garage wearing denim overalls. He was a broad man with a face like my dad's and uncle's, framed with perfectly smoothed grey hair. My aunt Ellen sort of introduced us; "That's your granddad," was how she put it, and that was that. She may have exchanged brief words with him, but the encounter was over before it started. I was eight. Growing up, my dad never spoke of his father except a couple of times. When the subject came up, my dad's entire attitude would change. I got the sense that there was unspoken tension in their relationship. Unfortunately, my grandfather would leave this earth without us formally meeting. When he passed, my dad announced as if he were reciting a Cardinals baseball game score. No emotions, no details, and need for us to attend the funeral. Dad droves south with his sister to attend the service, but that would be the last time he was mentioned. I recalled thinking how sad it must have been to have lived and died without getting to know your grandchildren.

Now Grandma Ellison was the exact opposite. Her heart was as big as her beautiful smile. The family came first. Her deep cherry-red skin directly affected her partial Native American roots. She had a mouth like a sailor. She was sharp as a razor, and her thick curly hair was often pulled to the crown of her head with the length hanging around the nape of her neck. She, too, wore dark-rimmed glasses that hid her beautiful slender face. Like Madear, Granny Ellison's doors often swung open with grandkids on the other side. My Aunt Eunice (my dad's sister) lived across the street with her six kids. There was a never-ending stream of repeat visitors in my grandma's house. My cousins and I ran in and out the front door, getting water and asking for money for ice cream, candy, and everything else. Grandma Ellison was more liberal than Madear, French (profanity) was her second language, she loved watching wrestling on television, and although we went to church, it was not mandatory. She drank beer and hung out with friends around the neighborhood. Although I cannot recall what she did for a living, she was independent.

I learned a lot from being close to both my paternal and maternal sides of the family. You can say I had the best of both worlds. Each side was sprinkled with humor, charm, and tenacity but was also plagued with its generational pathologies. To sum it up, I had more than enough love, cousins, playtime, and freedom to be a kid. I will forever be grateful for those essentials, which provided a solid foundation.

The things I missed would prove more necessary as years passed and I encountered life on my terms. Things like effectively communicating, integrity, and acceptance. The things I built never lasted; the cracks in my foundation would always prove too massive to sustain the structures I was attempting to build. The words "I love you" or "love you" were almost taboo in our house. Although my parents never said it, it was understood and displayed through their actions, discipline, and genuine interest in our well-being. We were blessed, but at times we were too selfish to see just how much. I spent too much time trying to get the things I did not have and not enough time appreciating the things I did. We lived in a simple one-story all-brick two-bedroom, one-bath home. My dad drove older-model vehicles, and our wardrobe was sparsely sprinkled with popular labels. My dad was conservative when it came to spending money, especially on brand-named items. He didn't understand all the fuss; a pair of shoes or pants was just that to him. At times, he would compromise with us. Instead of picking our clothes during back-to-school shopping, sometimes he would say, "Now you got $150, you can either get one outfit or more, but once it's spent … that's it." I knew he just wanted us to make good choices, but good choices had little to do with keeping up with the trends.

One Christmas, I only wanted a pair of Marc Albert rider boots. They were all the rave. I had to go back to school after winter break with those boots. So, on Christmas Eve, my dad drove around in the snow to three different malls to find the right size and color to make me happy. He had some choice words on the drive, but he ultimately wanted to ensure I got the one thing I wanted. I was thrilled that my dad would pay $98 for one pair of boots. He said, "For ninety-eight dollars, these boots better go with everything you have." That moment was so special for two reasons. One, my dad was involved. And secondly, it was one of a few times when I got exactly what I wanted without compromise. That was what winning felt like: the right designer, color, and style. Everything was in alignment…perfection. I still did not have enough stylist shit to be voted "best dressed" or anything, but I was over the moon about my boots. Thanks for that memory, Dad.

PLANS

The US census bureau reports that black families living in poverty in 1989 (the year I got the boots) were 29.7 percent. We were not one of those families. The absence of designer labels was one thing but having our needs met, and some of our wants were saying a mouthful. Like many parents, ours kept us active, and it must have cost them a small fortune to keep three kids in gymnastics, swimming, dance, football, tee-ball, track, and modeling.

My first love was gymnastics. I remember watching the Moscow Olympics in 1980 and being inspired by Nadia' performance. She was 18 but had made history in the '76 Olympics by becoming the first woman to score a perfect 10 in an Olympic event. I was drawn to her excellence and ability to capture the audience on the world stage. I was captivated by her every move, and it was then, at the tender age of eight, that I knew what I wanted to do. Whatever she had that made an entire crowd of more than 20,000 people hold their breath (not including the millions watching TV), I wanted some of that magic. This was not a here today, gone tomorrow kind of dream, I was still in love with the sport four years later at the 1984 Olympics when Mary Lou Retton tumbled her way into the history books as well.

Not long after the Olympics of '84, my parents enrolled my brothers and me in gymnastics at our local YMCA. My first pursuit of happiness began. I worked hard and was never bothered by after school or Saturday practice. Sabrina and Mark were dedicated coaches who once dreamt of a chance to perform and compete in this graceful and disciplined sport. I had fun and shared my dream of one day going to the Olympics with anyone that would listen. I mistakenly shared my aspiration with my favorite aunt on a Sunday ride home from church. Her reply was unexpected. "Gymnastics? child, your betta, find you a job that pays; you can't make no money doing flips." It was a stick pin to my bubble. I was devastated. I wanted to do what I loved and provide for my family. I decided to keep my freaking dreams to myself going forward. But if what she said was true, I had to rethink some things.

My parents spent considerable time supporting our dreams and everything else. After my Olympic dreams were shot, I moved on to a career in modeling. My dad reluctantly enrolled me at John Robert Powers Modeling Agency. I did a few showcases and some live window display jobs but nothing significant. I thought modeling would provide a way to interact with like-minded people, see the world and stay fresh and beautiful. I lived vicariously through the pages of my favorite magazines. *Seventeen*, *Young Miss* for fashion, then *Word Up!* and *Right On!* for popular trends. My idols were Whitney Houston and Madonna. I wanted to sing like Whitney and own my sexuality like the self-proclaimed "Material Girl" herself. I dreamt of moving to New York City and getting friendly with celebrities, if not becoming one myself. I worked to stay physically fit, and I took advice from the pages of the above magazines.

Having perfect skin, pretty teeth, and a thin frame was what I saw in magazines when I was growing up. No big asses and wide hips, no extra-large breasts (except Dolly Parton), and the most common plastic surgery was rhinoplasty (nose job) and breast implants (for the flat-chested). The people I aspired to look like were just pretty girlnext-door types. Not fake and overdone. Celebrities graced our screens while models graced our magazine covers ... imagine that. I grew up in the best era ever! My generation created hip hop, made Whitney Houston an icon, introduced Mariah Carey, and had just as many British bands on the Billboard as American ones. I am sure my parents thought we were too progressive with our music, choice in fashion, and cable TV. The difference between then and now, we had a choice. There were just as many positive images and music as negative or destructive ones in the media.

For ages, African Americans have been portrayed as criminals, uneducated, lazy, violent, and unattractive (unless you were damn near white). But our videos and commercials had a fair proportion of darker and fair-skinned people. We had Salt-N-Pepa, Lauryn Hill and Lisa Bonet, Kid and Play, Wesley Snipes, and Allen Payne. Our music was either empowering or perverted. Either you listened to Boogie Down Production and Queen Latifah or preferred the harder and more sexual lyrics of NWA and Oaktown 3.5.7. There was just enough information about famous people, not 24-hour news. No blatant body shamming. No reality shows, and no one was paid and praised for being "*just* pretty". There were commercials for baby dolls and racetracks. Kids watched cartoons every Saturday morning and *The Three Stooges* on Saturday night. Our Christmas list consisted of Atari, action figures, life-sized Barbie Dream homes, and the infamous Cabbage Patch dolls. Our era ushered in the best African American television show of all time—the *Cosby Show*; we played on the first computers (we had the Commodore 64), and games like Pac-Mac, Centipede, and Donkey Kong captured our attention for hours. Penny candy was still a penny, and big-screen TVs took up entire wall. What a blast I had growing up in the '80s. This generation also encountered its plethora of problems; with hip hop came explicit lyrics, where the words bitch, and nigga replaced sir and ma'am. The explosive teenage pregnancy rate was being discussed nationally, and crack, and mandatory prison sentences probably destroyed more black families than slavery. This was my foundation. Generation X baby: take it or leave it.

You're welcome.

WHERE IS SHE?!

With all my teenage wants, a sister was at the top of the list. She was part of that move to New York City and model daydream I used to have. Yeah, I had my cousins, but a sister would be better than a friend because our bond would be unbreakable, right? These dreams were fueled by the news that I had a half-sister, Joseline. I found this out when I was around 12 or 13. I pumped; my very own sister? We could dress up like the girls in my favorite magazines and arrange our bedroom like an apartment. I couldn't ask for a greater gift. I forgot about all the crap I had taken from my cousin Dawn. I was moving on to bigger and better things with my own flesh and blood. Things were looking up. What could go wrong?

Before the news of my sister, my cousin Tamika was a sister to me. She was my best friend. We shared and talked about everything. Tamika was a bit of a brat with no real discipline and enough attitude for both of us. But I loved her and enjoyed her company. I could share all my dreams with her. Yeah, she was rough around the edges, but she was real. We had many of the same interests and got along great for the most part. My deeply rooted desire to have a sister with whom to share my life made me a little possessive at times. This irritated the hell out of Tamika, and then she would demand to go home, but once I gave her some space, we were back to being two peas in a pod. As the years passed, we grew apart, but she has always remained my first ride-or-die chick.

Anyway, when I got the news about Joseline, I made space for her in the closet, changed the room around, cleared out drawers, and put out the latest magazines so we could come up with a theme for our room together. Since I was the oldest, I should at least have things planned. Not once did I stop to think about what she liked or wanted. I wanted her to fit into my ideal role, which was probably my first mistake. I was over the moon with excitement and questions for my parents. "When can I meet her?" "When is her birthday?" "Where does she live?" "When is she moving in?" And so forth. It was easier to get answers from my mom than from my dad. See, Joseline was younger than me and older than Kei. You do the math. It was probably a less-than-proud moment for my parents, but no shame in bringing a beautiful daughter into the world. On the contrary, how my mom embraced Joseline protected us from any past or future drama a lesser woman would have allowed. Behind closed doors, I am sure my mom had moments regarding the infidelity at some point, but if she had any hard feelings about it, she could have won an Academy Award for not showing it.

There was quite a lag in time from hearing about Joseline and the day we met. But the day I found out she was coming; I re-did everything. I arranged and then rearranged my room and did rigorous workouts (so I could be in tip-top shape); I reorganized my closet, styled my hair differently, and brushed up on all the articles in my current magazines. I wanted to converse about fashion and makeup like a pro. After all, I had to make an impeccable first impression.

I cannot remember what my brothers were doing the day she arrived, but my dad was sitting on the couch facing the bay window, watching television. My mom kept pacing back and forth from the living room to the kitchen, where she was putting the final touches on a meal she had prepared for the occasion. Finally, I heard her shout, "They're here!" My heart started to race and pound so hard that I thought I would collapse. Instead, I took a deep breath and joined my mom as she briskly walked back into the living room from the kitchen. The blinds were open so I could see my cousin, who had driven Joseline to our home, as she walked across the street. I made it my mission not to look out the window at my sister. I did not want to spoil that first impression moment. I was so caught in my thoughts that I didn't notice my mom had come to a complete stop. I was so close I stepped on the back of her shoes. As I backed up to give my mom some space, I caught a glimpse of a girl who was supposedly my sister, walking across the street with my cousin.

The first thing I noticed was her demeanor and then her clothes. Was this Joseline or someone else? When they entered the house, my dad rose to greet them, and my mom and cousin embraced. I stood there for a minute, trying to take it all in. She was pretty, but we barely made eye contact. The best way to describe that moment was finally going on vacation, only to find out it would rain the entire time you were there. You are still on vacation but must adjust your expectations and plans. My energy wavered from elation to wishful to solemn within moments; my plans to dress alike, travel the world, and be best friends seemed farther than China as we exchanged short glances. I wondered if she, too, was a fan of fashion magazines. Did she have a boyfriend? Was she as neat as me? Would we get along? I wanted to go to my room, nap, and sleep it off. Hopefully, this was all a dream, and my real sister would arrive soon. I kept waiting for them to say this was someone other than Joseline, but no such thing happened. To this date, we have not formed a sisterly bond. I love my baby sis, but neither of us got past our first impression of each other on that fateful day. I wondered what she expected. Maybe her demeanor changed when she saw me. Who knows? Over the years, my sister and I have formed a cordial relationship but nothing more.

She was closer to my brothers than to me. From my perspective, there was no bad blood but no connection.

Surprisingly, Joseline and my mom had the tightest bond. They spoke often and visited one another, and because of their relationship, the rest of us could stay abreast of all things Joseline.

From what I was told, Joseline's mother was killed in an automobile accident when she was very young. After her mother's passing, Joseline went to live with her mom's sister. I also understand that Joseline came into a large sum of money she would have access to when she turned 21 or married, she got married right after high school.

I remember visiting my sisters' new townhouse, decked with custom furniture and new clothes. She was big on jewelry, so she and hubby stayed blinged in gold rings, earrings, and necklaces. To top it off, they purchased the newly introduced four-door, Chevy Blazer. My baby sis had it going on. I was so impressed and proud of her. But that would be short-lived. I have learned that a lack of knowledge about money management can create more problems than the lack of money itself. I just assumed my sister would be balling forever. The opportunity to brag about her accomplishments made me feel good. Selfish.

My dad was a great money manager because of his old-school frugal mentality. I recall a conversation I overheard him have with my mom about reaching out to Joseline to help her save her money, which he followed up with, "She is grown, and she refused my offer to help." He was more than a little upset that the powers that be gave such a young person so much at once. He knew the money would run through her fingers like water. He was right. Without legal rights, he had to sit back and watch his baby girl make a mess of a once-in-a-lifetime opportunity to change the financial trajectory or her life and the lives of her children. There is no doubt that we shared the same bloodline, Joseline and I. Over the years following her windfall, she would experience abuse, divorce, legal issues, and brokenness. Yet today, she is traveling the country ministering to others. Our lives have taken similar paths without being raised in the same household. She has written a book, purchased a home, raised her children, gotten degrees, climbed the medical field ladder, and is a respectably sought-after speaker. She is one of my greatest personal inspirations, and to call her "sister" is an honor. Hopefully, one day soon, I can call her "friend."

BROTHERS

My brothers, Kei, and Kame, what a pair. Thirteen months apart, they were often mistaken as twins. Spoiled and pampered. When they arrived, it was all about these two little ones. It was time for me to be a big sis. As a baby, Kei was hairy and beautiful and didn't cry much. He was chill and has remained that way his entire life. Even when he and Kame were mischievous, I am sure he was the manipulator. But he kept it low-key. Growing up, I dreaded watching them while my parents went shopping or ran errands. They were so bad they would gang up on me and start shit all the time. Looking back, they were not so bad; I had no patience. Compared to some of the horror stories shared by others, my baby brothers were angels. However, at the time, picking at each other and fighting was a bit much for me. I shouldn't complain; I used to make them act like my kids when playing house, which frustrated the hell out of them both. On the flip side, as they got older, we saw the value in having siblings, and the hours playing board games, racing our bikes, or taking in the scenery on road trips with our parents made great memories.

The baby of the bunch was my wide-eyed, fat-cheeked, cry baby brother Kame. From he came home from the hospital until now, he has made his presence known. Kame was the vocal one, and because of that, we bumped heads more than Kei, and I did. We had a lot in common, vocal, and rebellious, for different reasons. Mine, because of trauma, was the view of his relationship with our dad. Kame felt he had to compete for the love he thought Kei received naturally. I saw some of the same things Kame complained about regarding my dad. However, as I matured and had my children, I understood that my dad gave each child what he thought they needed from him. Some kids must figure things out independently, while others need constant guidance and nurturing. Where Kame saw neglect, it was just my dad giving him space to be the decisive, talented, smart, and outgoing person who thrives when he thinks no one is looking. In contrast, Kei needed reassurance and more direction from my dad to get things started, but once he got going, he always excelled.

Slow, steady, reliable, talented, and wise words to describe Kei. Like taking the high road and living above the influence of a lot of bullshit, he could have found himself involved in. He is not a saint, but his character precedes him, and I am especially proud of the person he has always been. As kids, we teach our parents how to treat us. No two kids are the same, and most parents do what they believe is most beneficial for that child. Some kids need lifting, while others need picking up. Kame needed picking up. He was the one who was always getting hurt, with a head hard as cement. His fearless behavior saw my parents save their energy for the reaction to Kame, whereas they spent time being proactive with Kei. The love is the same, just distributed differently.

I was so caught up with my boyfriends, drinking and partying, that I missed some of their teenage milestones. However, I smile remembering the first time I called home, and one of them answered the phone sounding like a man. It was cool and hilarious to see them grow up. My friends and I used to joke about it all the time. Although I was not always around, I knew what was happening. Plus, I hope the years spent cheering them on and supporting them as they played every sport helped to express how much I love them. Finally, I hope my absence did not convey abandonment. After all, I could not have been blessed with a cooler pair of young men to call my brothers.

MORE PLANS

Silk was the name of our singing group/band. This was the beginning of middle school, and I was deeply committed—yet again—to my new career choice. An R&B singer. I told you Whitney Houston, and Madonna were my idols, right? In middle school, I participated in talent shows every chance I got. I thought I could sing like Whitney, be sexy like Madonna, and move like Janet. I'm sure it was a delusion, but it was a great time to be an adolescent. Back then, we could sing most of our favorite songs out loud (no explicit labels) around adults without getting into trouble. I convinced six friends to join me on this epic adventure to become stars. I promised them that if we worked hard and wrote great songs, we could be the female New Edition. I wrote songs like "Lovers Delight" and "Candy Boy." We had no sense of music or how to write it, but I figured we were headed to the Grammy's since I had a drum set and ambition. So, with parental approval, every Saturday, Cali, Joy, Charmin, Vivian, and two others I can't remember, and I piled into my parents' modest living room for a two-hour jam session. At one rehearsal, Joy (our designated drummer) used my mom's candlesticks as her drumsticks, and I was livid. Our time together was a joke; we spent more time arguing about the songs than singing them. My first attempt at funding the group was selling candy at school to raise money for equipment and outfits. A little over a month into the rehearsals, I had more success making money selling candy than we did as a group. Those girls played too much, I was trying to do something great, and they saw it as an opportunity to hang out on Saturday. Commitment is half the battle, and that is what we lacked. I disband the group in search of greener pastures after three rehearsals. I guessed I would keep trying new things until I found something that worked.

Over the summers, I read and thumbed through books at the local library. At one point, I thought about becoming an attorney, but that soon gave way to becoming a famous writer. I even got one of my writings published in a teen magazine once. No compensation or anything. At the time, magazines encouraged readers to send in their take on stories or suggestions for topics to discuss. I submitted my reply to an article in story form. Then I got lucky. I checked each publication carefully to see whose comments or articles made it for that month. Then, finally, after months of anticipation, I saw it; F. Ellison, St. Louis, MO, graced the page in small letters following my written response. I felt the world would read that little paragraph, and opportunities would flow in all directions. No correspondence, phone calls, or urgent requests for me to pack up and move to New York followed. I didn't make a big fuss over it either, I shared the article with my mom, and that was that. Yet, it was enough to let me know that even I, from my princess-themed decorated bedroom in St. Louis, could grab the attention of editors in New York City. Kind of.

Even before this small publication, I wrote incessantly. Writing has always been a form of therapy for me. I wrote down my feelings, my doubts, fears, and plans. When I disagreed with my mom, I would curse and threaten her on paper. Reading and writing were always comforting to me. Reading allowed me to travel to places and experience things mentally that I never did physically. It gave me insight into how different ages and ethnic groups thought and lived. Reading took me away from problems and allowed me to escape for a few hours. Reading also fostered dreams and imagination I might have missed if I had not read. I took the opportunity to write out a checklist of sorts for my life: First things first, get accepted into Hampton University; graduate;

get a job offer; move to New York City; meet and marry a professional athlete; have one or two kids; live lavishly and travel the world ... the end. Maybe I had seen too many Disney movies. Although my plans were attainable, they were shallow. Whoever said, "What you do today will show up in your life tomorrow," knew exactly what they were talking about. Almost every choice I made from that point on led me in the opposite direction than the one I wrote about.

AND SO, IT BEGINS

University City high school was nothing short of a great time. I would not change that experience for anything in the world. Well, maybe some parts of it. I participated in anything I could. Track, softball, cheerleading, pompom, flag squad, SADD, yearbook; you name it, I did it. I won homecoming court in my junior year and homecoming queen in my senior year. I was a 2.9 GPA student who could have put forth better effort to achieve a higher ranking. I could have excelled academically if it were not for such a healthy social life. Priorities.

I met my best friend/sister Tai in the seventh grade. We shared home economics. I was sort of a class clown, and one day, during a brief lesson on penmanship, I went to the board and outlined my hand, then labeled it "TALL hand" and drew an image of a small hand and labeled it "short-hand." I do not know why but Tai thought that was the funniest thing she ever saw. Thirty-three years later, she is still laughing at my jokes. My right-hand man (or woman). We have had our share of laughs, cries, triumphs, and tragedies.

In the ninth grade, Cali joined us. It was—Tai, Cali, Viv, Penny, Kiara, Toni, Laney, Cassie, Tabitha, and Nikki. From break-ups to unplanned pregnancies, we shared some of the most memorable moments a four-year stint would allow. Within our large group, a smaller one was created. That smaller group consisted of me, Tai, Cali, and Viv (sisters). Their mothers were my second moms. Gia and Sandra.

I have nothing but nostalgia when I reflect on my wonder years. I recall getting dressed up for our school dances on Friday nights. I thought I was the shit, sporting Guess jeans, a washed-silk shirt, and Etienne Aigner ankle boots. There were no MAC cosmetics, but Fashion Fair had a great line of makeup for women of color. Chocolate raspberry lipstick was the most popular. Giorgio Armani Red was my scent of choice, and Liz Claiborne had the popular purses for my price point. We walked into school dances with the confidence of the Victoria's Secret runway model. School dances were held in the larger gym on campus. Pack a bunch of hormone-crazed kids in a smelly venue, add a DJ, and you have a party. What a great time. Other than the bullshit I encountered when my boyfriend decided to cheat on me, my memory of this period fills me with happiness.

We were the University City Indians, or U. City Indians for short. The team with the black and gold. Although it was a majority black student body, our school was a melting pot. In earlier years, University City was a predominately Jewish community. Unlike many of the modern, office park-type construction schools you see nowadays, University City High is a beautifully designed school with architectural details that I believe would rival monuments that people travel to see. I could be exaggerating, but the outside was nice. As with most high schools, your sense of pride came from a rich heritage mostly based on sports performance and records. We were no different; sports were a big deal for our high school. And there was no time like a homecoming weekend to show your school spirit. The schedule went as follows: Pep rally during school on Friday and a bonfire later that night, where everyone wore school colors or their letterman jackets or uniform shirt (if you played a sport). Everyone would gather at Heman Park, just down the street from the high school. The cheerleaders, flag squad, and pom-pom teams would perform cheers around the bonfire. People participated; we hyped ourselves up and talked shit about the opposing team for the next day's homecoming battle. We danced, mingled, and had a blast.

Saturday, we participated in the homecoming parade. The parade started in the U. City loop and continued a little under two miles to the high school. I was on the cheerleading squad my freshman and sophomore year, and for the other two years, I was homecoming court (junior year) and homecoming queen (senior) year. As a part of the homecoming court, you rode on a float or in a car and waved to the bystanders. The streets were littered with people, and the energy was and still is what bonds this community. Waving, cheering, socializing, dancing, and eating was great time. But, of course, the big game was after the parade, and we wrapped the festivities up with our infamous homecoming dance later that night.

Everyone should experience high school to the fullest. I need to shout my parents out for settling in such a rich, diverse, cool-ass part of town. I remember during basketball season how exciting it was to play against popular "city" schools. The rest of the world would call them "ghettos," but we called the city schools "city" (schools located in the metropolitan district of St. Louis). To us, these kids looked, dressed, and acted ghetto but were talented as hell. We went to the extreme of being disrespectful. I recall, Jeri curl caps being passed out to students one Friday during school. Later that night, during the game, as the competing team was being announced, our entire side of the gym pulled out those plastic curl caps and put them on. It was a symbol of disrespect and how we viewed them. Jeri Curl=one of the black hair trends that gave our hair the appearance and feel of soft natural curls, was extremely popular, especially in the "city". Damn!

Reflecting on the joke, it was fucked up. Almost racist. If we were a school full of white students, we would have made national news. No wonder other schools felt some type of way about U. City. We didn't care; we were the U. City Indians and proud of it. If I could go back today, I would. But life does not move in that direction, even though experiences may. Some of my most fond memories occurred in high school. I learned to multitask, be aggressive, speak Spanish, and play sports; I fell in love for the first time, had my heart broken for the first time, and got my first alcohol assessment. Yup, you read right. My first alcohol assessment.

BOYZ TO MEN

My first love and heartbreak came in the same package. His name was Galvin Tombs. He was my high school sweetheart and my friend. Tall, nice body, handsome, chocolate, and dapper. From the start, we were inseparable. His friends were my friends and vice versa. I truly had the biggest crush on him while we were dating. I felt like a priority, beautiful, respected, and special in that relationship. We spent so much time together. Then, in our sophomore year, I started to get that urge to create a deeper bond. I wanted to have sex. I wanted to experience intimacy on my terms with the man I was in love with. No deceit, no manipulation, just two young people in love. Sex would be an enormous step for us. Hell, in the beginning, it took over two weeks before our first tongue kiss. I patiently waited for him to work up the nerves to initiate it. It was the sweetest thing when it finally happened. We hung around the cafeteria talking after school one day, and he leaned in and gave me the best first kiss ever. I miss the innocence of those moments when it was okay to be coy and respectful.

It is no surprise that Galvin was taken aback by my bold confession that I wanted to add sex into the relationship. Honestly, I think he wanted to be the one to bring it up. But I was too naive to understand that. Believe it or not, he was not ready to have sex, and our opposing views were enough to end the relationship. While apart, Galvin started dating Cassie Shepard, a feisty young lady with street smarts and a one-year-old child. She was a year behind us in high school, but she was leap years ahead of most people her age. I liked them together, and I thought they made a cute couple.

We both had moved on, and I was confident he was no longer a virgin, dating a girl with a child. So, it came as no surprise towards the end of our junior year when Galvin started coming around and making a case for us to give our relationship another attempt. I always had respect for him and cared about him. So, if he was no longer seeing Cassie, I was open to having another go at it, as he suggested. When we made it official before the beginning of our senior year, it was like we had not missed a beat. Things were great, and then one Friday night, we were headed out to see a movie. As we approached the mall, Galvin commented about skipping the movie so we could explore our conversation from a couple of years earlier. I had not mentioned sex since we had been back together and was caught off guard that Galvin was the initiator. So instead of turning into the mall parking lot, he went straight and headed towards the National Lodge, where we would consummate our relationship. I blushed at the thought of how things had changed within such a short time. He was a gentleman, and that first time together solidified that I had made a good choice in him. We were following a natural course, friends then lovers.

My senior year was the most memorable of high school, but for all the wrong reasons. The highlights included making lifelong friendships, being crowd homecoming court in my junior year and homecoming queen in my senior year, marching in the Mardi Gras parade with my school's band, the cheerleading and pompom squad, running track, punk rock fashion, boom boxes, hip hop, and enough laughs to last three lifetimes. The downside was the relationship with Galvin I thought so highly of, for it would test me in ways no teenage girl should be tested.

My boyfriend was not completely honest with me on our second try; he and Cassie were still seeing each other. Suddenly my life, both public and personal, took an unexpected turn for the worse. One day, upon my arrival at school, a fellow student approached me and asked if I had been to the cafeteria already. "Well, no!" I said, seeing that I had just walked into the building. "What's up?" I was taken aback by her eagerness to inform me of the impeding troubles that day would bring. As it turns out, Galvin's other woman had put up posters in the school cafeteria with the caption, "Fatou Ellison and Galvin Tombs are stupid as fuck; she is pregnant." She made a point of including both of our full names. I am sure everyone would have known us without the last names for clarity.

Once again, my privacy had been violated. This was the Instagram post of my day. Poster board in a public place. What a jealous ass vengeful bitch. Vengeful or not, it was the truth. Yup, that is right; I was pregnant and hiding it. It never occurred to me how she could be confident about her statements. Thinking back, it was Galvin who spilled the beans. Hell, I was less than five weeks at the time; I was not showing and had not shared this information with anyone but him and Tai. I wish I could say that shit storm came and went without damage, but I would be lying. This was only the start of a tsunami that would rip apart the remainder of my senior year and beyond. Cassie turned underclassmen against me as she convinced them that I had it out for her. And suddenly, Miss Well-Liked became public enemy number one. I was seventeen, pregnant, confused, nauseous, and watching my back. All of this before the first bell rang.

After first period, Cassie and her followers threatened me (I had no idea what she or the other bitches were talking about). "Im'ma beat this, and we gonna beat that" was all I recall hearing. Until then, Cassie and I had never spoken to each other. There was never any uneasiness between us, so this baffled me. I guess the thought of me having her man's baby pushed her over the edge, and she became obsessed with my demise, to which I replied, "Why are you fucking with *me*? *Fuck* with Galvin." At that point, things got out of control. I started getting belligerent phone calls, physical intimidation, and damage to personal property. I was living a real-life fatal attraction. This bitch needed a hug or a fucking role model. There was no way I liked/loved/gave a fuck about anyone enough at that age to go through all of this.

In the end, Galvin and I would have children ... just not with each other. The baby that became the topic of our cafeteria chatter was aborted six weeks into my term. That same week my dad overheard me cursing Galvin over the phone one evening. I must have been in my feelings because I held nothing back. Galvin was on the other end trying to convince me to keep the baby and move in with his cousin who played for the San Francisco 49ers, get married and start a new life. While I protested his suggestions, I disclosed that I was pregnant loud enough for my parents to hear. Of course, the whole house could hear my frustrations bouncing off the hard wood floors, telling my boyfriend why I did not want to end up like his ex or whatever she was to him. Thinking back, it might not have been such a bad idea. Who knows what might have happened?

That night, after my dad left for work and my brothers were asleep, my mom came into my room and stood in my doorway. I had no idea why she looked like she had just lost her best friend until she said, "So you're pregnant, Fatou?" At that moment, I understood the look on her face was ... hopelessness. Her greatest fear had come true. Her only daughter repeats the dreaded act of having kids too young. Growing up, my mom would always say things like, "Don't get pregnant," "You don't want to have kids before you get married," and "Don't make the same mistakes I made." With her bold question, everything I felt about my situation came out in the form of tears. My mom ran over to console me as I wept. I was so ashamed, confused, and disappointed. She was angry at me but used Galvin as her target instead. She blamed him for everything, but I knew better. Her real anger was at me, and the things she left out of her rant were heard louder than she included.

I could not fall asleep that night, so I lay on the couch. I must have drifted off because I was startled by a ringing phone around 3:00 a.m.; it was my dad. As soon as I answered, he asked, "So you're pregnant?" I didn't respond. My dad went to work at

11:00 p.m. He must have contemplated how he would address my "situation" during the hours leading up to the 3:00 a.m. call. He called to speak to me only when he had convinced himself of an acceptable solution. It just happened to be at 3:00 a.m. on a school night. He told me how this would play out in the upcoming weeks; I was instructed that I would get to school late that morning because we were going to Planned Parenthood. Damn, it was obvious where I got the take charge attitude; dad had figured things out without my input. But there was no way in hell I was going to protest. Plus, I had no idea what Planned Parenthood was, but I was going to find out.

Later that morning, we went to Planned Parenthood; I did not take one breath until I found out what my dad was arranging. At first, I thought he was setting me up with parental training, but I realized that Planned Parenthood performed abortions. I probably should not have been so relieved, but I was. I had no intentions of being a mother before graduation, if at all. We had a consultation and set things in motion. After all, I had no energy to deal with the backlash and harassment at school that was sure to come if I carried the baby to term. Things were unraveling, and the Galvin situation had gotten dangerously out of hand. One night, we (me, Galvin, Tai, Daniel, and Luke P) were headed to a school dance. When we turned onto the street to our school, Galvin's headlights caught a glimpse of what seemed to be a mob of people congregating alongside the school building. Not sure what they were up to, we soon got our answer as things quickly escalated. When the mob realized it was Galvin's truck, they hastily pursued it. They swarmed us like bees, yelling obscenities for me to get out of the truck, saying, "fuck me this" and "fuck me that." What the hell was going on? Then I saw her, the ringleader. Cassie appeared at the front of the truck, demanding Galvin get out or they would destroy his beloved vehicle.

Dead silence fell over the inside of the truck as we watched the people, we were cool with earlier that day, waiting for a chance to kick us in the face or something. With each passing moment, the crowd grew more aggressive. They were kicking, screaming, and waiting to get their hands on us. They started rocking the truck then someone kicked the door. That was enough for him to announce that he would start running motherfuckers over if they didn't move out of his way. The demands for him to deliver me to the crowd intensified as Galvin and Daniel jumped out of the truck and locked the doors. I was sitting in the passenger seat thinking, *Sure, I'll get out and get my pretty ass beat by a mob of drunken teenagers ... no thank you!* When he opened the door, the mob looked like roaches when the lights come on, scattering into the open spaces to get at Tai and me. Galvin maneuvered to the best of his ability to thwart their efforts. I'd done absolutely nothing to these bitches. I was guilty of being in a relationship with a dishonest man, so why was I going through hell? I was thinking, *Hell, just fuck him up while he's out there and leave me alone.* I figured Cassie was just jealous that it didn't work out between her and Galvin, and she wanted to see nothing more than our relationship fail (kid or not).

When Galvin got out of the truck, she was the first one in his face, pushing him and yelling in his face! Fatou who? It was like I wasn't even there. Pop, pop, pop... Shots rang out and broke the blank star on my face watching this BS take place. It was Tanya Portland's fat ass, shooting in the air to disperse the crowd and get some attention. Galvin jumped back in the truck and sped away as the crowd darted in different directions for protection. We never made it to the dance that night. The fun night we had planned was ruined by the secrets of the man sitting next to me. The ride to grab something to eat and then home was quiet as hell.

Later that week, my brothers and I sat at the dining room table doing homework. My dad was on the couch watching TV when we heard a loud crashing sound at our front window. My dad jumped up and headed outside to see what was going on. There was a chip in our bay window, and laughter ensued in the distance. My dad must have spotted the culprits because the next thing we knew, he was barefoot and bare-chested chasing them. My brothers and I ran to the front porch to see which direction they ran and to be witnesses to the crime our father was surely about to commit. We were concerned about the poor soul that threw the bottle at our window. If my dad caught them, there would be hell to pay. Things like this became more frequent since Cassie made it her personal goal to ruin my life.

One afternoon, my dad sat me down and said, "Fatou, I know you don't want to hear this, but the only reason that girl is messing with you is that Galvin is still messing around with her." You should have seen my reaction. It was like someone had told me I only had 48 hours to live. I was in disbelief. I stormed out of the house and ran to Tai's place. As soon as she opened her door, I told her what my dad had shared. Her facial expression displayed confusion, and, just like me, I am sure the possibility of Galvin still fooling around with his ex was hard to believe for her as well. I mean, damn, when did he find the time? The tears that lined the crease of my eyes fought to stay inside, but the thought of being fooled was more than my childish heart could fathom. I cried like a baby as my best friend tried to reason with me. After the tears came anger, so I confronted Galvin about all the stuff Cassie was doing and why, to which he laid on the charm and had me fully convinced that I was the only woman for him. Of course, Cassie wanted to get back together, but as he pointed out on numerous occasions, I was the one he wanted to be with, or else he would not have broken up with her. That was all I needed to hear. After that conversation, I was back on his team.

Fast forward two weeks. My friends and I were hanging out at Forest Park on a typical Sunday afternoon. Forest Park was the place to be on a Sunday, with beautiful people, expensive cars, and expensive sound systems, St. Louis's hottest came out on Sunday to see and be seen. Dope dealers, hustlers, gang bangers, college kids, baby mommas, baby daddies, and perpetrators packed the park. Cars and people as far as the eyes could see. The base from the cars' boom boxes was so loud that it altered your heartbeat and made you gasp for air. For us, this was between 1:00 p.m. and dark, after which you went and got changed for Saints, one of our popular skating rinks. It was the second place to see and be seen on Sundays. No other day of the week provided such a buffet of heavily attended gatherings. I loved Sundays. However, this Sunday, neither Tai nor the crew went to the skating rink with me; instead, I rode with Cali and her then boyfriend, Jimmy.

On the way home, I asked Jimmy to drive down 28th Street; I had an awful suspicion that I wanted to prove wrong. Twenty-Eighth Street was where Luke P lived, and since no one from our crew was spotted at the rink, I wanted to see if everyone was gathered at Luke P's house. When we rode past, I saw everyone's vehicle parked outside except Galvin's. I asked Jimmy to make a left onto Cassie's Street for my peace of mind (she lived about three blocks up from Luke P). As luck would have it, as soon as he turned left onto her street, the reflection of Galvin's blue truck and exaggerated tire rims sat like the prelude to a horror movie. My heart sank into my stomach, and I could not breathe. Wow! After all the shit that had gone down between me, Cassie and Galvin, my dad was right.

At that moment, I got a good taste of what betrayal felt like. Ten years after my cousin took my innocence, my first love had taken my trust. He could have cheated with anyone else in St. Louis, but his choice confirmed that people are selfish and capable of the worst things imaginable. In that same moment, I understood what murders meant when they speak of things going black, and you wake up without recollecting what happened. I know, for a split second, the world had no sound, and I was left with my adrenaline and aching heart, both leaving me empty of sound judgment. It was as if I had an out-of-body experience. I clawed my way out from the backseat of Jimmy's sedan, trying to get to Galvin, get fresh air, get out; to witness my first love and his other woman together after a school year of terror was an overly dramatic way to validate my dad's revelations a couple of weeks earlier. As I pushed passed the driver of my vehicle, I began yelling obscenities and threats. Galvin's dumb ass looked like a deer in headlights ... stunned. He made a lame attempt to address me, but it was like watching a movie with the sound off. I could not hear or interpret anything coming from his lips. Everything that was occurring seemed to be in slow motion. Cassie kept pulling Galvin back towards her and demanding he go inside her house. I assumed that was the exchange of words based on her body language and his escape inside her house. Jimmy and Cali were playing referee and pulling me in the opposite direction. What a night! not only was I finding that out in real time, one of my closet friends and her guy were witnessing it too.

The images of my man and another woman on the same side of this conflict became etched into my memory forever. It is what hurt the most. From that point on, this display from my deceitful lover and his side chick would lay the foundation for me to exist in relationships. It was more than sex with Galvin (or so I thought); he was my friend, and I trusted him. Up to this point, I had never been so humiliated; I would have chosen to fall into the school gutter ten more times place of this. I had been a friend to Galvin, I had been faithful and open to experiencing new things with him, and I had been respectful. Yet that did not stop my bae from running game on me. It would be the last time I offered all those things in a relationship. The tears I cried did little to console my soul and ego. I had gambled my trust for the lure of love and lost both.

I withdrew internally as Cali helped me back in the car, as I had nothing left after seeing Galvin's reaction. However, I wanted to see the guys at Luke P's house. I was convinced they had watched this overcrowded relationship run its course without giving me any heads-up. I ran through Luke P's backyard, through his kitchen door and down the basement steps. All the fellows were gathered in his basement. I felt so stupid, these were my homies, and it seemed like everyone in the world knew what was happening but me. It was like they felt it coming because no one would make eye contact. The chickens had come home to roost ... at my expense. I began crying and yelling at the guys, "How come you didn't tell me? I know you motherfuckers knew he was messing around with her!" The sound of people not breathing filled the room, and it was so quiet you could hear the ants crawling in the grass outside. Although I was putting them in the same awkward situation that my now ex-boyfriend had put me in, I wanted some answers, which Luke P, Daniel, Chris, and Tone could not provide.

In hindsight, I should not have allowed that incident to turn me into the person I became—hardened, unfaithful, suspicious of everyone, and on guard in relationships. I was too young to become cynical, but age never stopped me before. It took a while to get that; Galvin was just a kid, and so was I. People make mistakes, and I shouldn't made what happen mean anything more. But I was not armed with that knowledge when it happened. I got over Galvin, but I held claim to the residue of the events from that night forward. I had taken on the persona of a serial killer. I would go on murdering my relationships and take away the scars and disappointment as trophies from each victim. After the breakup with Galvin, I swore never to be faithful again. This would be the one vow that would remain unbroken for far too long.

In my senior year of high school, I applied to Hampton University in Virginia and LSU in New Orleans. My dad spoke to me about staying in St. Louis for my first two years. He offered to pay for me to get through community college. He reasoned that it would save a shit load of money to do the remedial course locally and then transfer to a university to complete my degree. I wanted to leave St. Louis, but with his financial sense and support, I knew I was making a solid decision. Therefore, I applied to Forest Park Community College and started my studies. I loved everything about being a college student. My BFF, Tai, decided she would get her associate degree and enrolled at Forest Park too.

Although they did not say it at first, I knew my parents were proud that their firstborn was leading the pack to higher learning. I worked hard, studied, and kept my social life in check. That said, Forest Park's curriculum was slightly harder than high school.

Nevertheless, I could complete assignments, research, and get reports done (at the last minute) while partying my ass off. After all, I was a college student. It didn't matter whether I stayed on campus or with my parents; the party never stopped.

While hanging out with friends one evening, I saw the most beautiful car I had ever seen. It was a sports car with a custom pearl-white paint job. Deep dish rims and clean as a whistle. While I was admiring the outside of the car, the driver was on the inside with admirations of his own. I used to have this thing for flashy men simply because they loved to spend money. And I loved to spend it too. So, when I was beckoned to come to the car to speak with the owner of this beautiful machine, and I happily strutted to his window. We exchanged numbers and agreed to follow up later the following day. He was not the most attractive man, but he had this confidence and swag about him that made up for it. And he fit the profile of the guys I liked. Hustlers. And by hustler, I mean just that. Drug dealers. They had respect, street credibility, balls, and money to burn. Mick was no exception. He was a whole lot cocky with a whole lot of cash.

We began a very casual relationship. That was it. That was all I needed—a guy who could hold his own, made a lot of money and said "Yes," to me way more than he said "No." The typical bad boy with a host of notorious associations. Don't judge. We all have had our share of bad boys. Mine was just bad in every way imaginable. I am not the only female attracted to men with power and money, so you know this relationship was never just between us. One of the side effects of dealing with a man of means and minimum moral values is his ability to accommodate others and his inability to stay committed. Mick was a father's nightmare for their daughter. He made an illegal living, was a known gang member, and had recently been released from jail, prison, or whatever on an alleged murder charge. The crazier thing is that this never deterred me from seeing him. Hell!

I was growing up in an era where drug dealers were hood celebrities. Yes, I was aware of the increased violence, prison sentences, and missing fathers, but somehow, I thought I could dip in, have fun, and get back to business when I was done. Not a chance; when you play with fire, you get burned. No need to blame the fire. This shit had become so commonplace that I was blind to the poison I supported through my attraction to easy money. To prevent my story from reading longer than it should, allow me to go in sequence to explain the web I was weaving for myself. A potentially dangerous one for all involved.

Enter TJ. I saw TJ and his friends on several occasions at the local skating rink. More than once, I also saw TJ being escorted out of that skating rink in handcuffs along with his crew for one altercation or another. He wasn't flashy, but he was known. He hailed from the Blumeyer's project, a popular housing development that produced some of Saint Louis's finest and, I do mean, fine men. So, when he came up to me at the skating rink and introduced himself, I naturally acted as if I had never seen him before. However, he was much calmer than I expected and had this confidence about himself.

Not cocky, just self-assured. We exchanged numbers, spoke for a minute, and he called later that night to ensure I had given him the right number. TJ, the fact-checker. He called the next day again and asked me out to dinner. I accepted, and we met later that week. Before the check came, he had made me his woman. Before I knew what had happened, I gave him my class schedule, so he knew when to pick me up from school. He was a man with a mission, and I was an actor in his play. One minute I was saying, "Let's just see where this goes," and the rest is history. True to his word, he was sitting in the parking lot the next day when we got out of class. He started scheduling things for us and we saw each other two or three times a week.

I lived with my parents, and he lived with his mom. Hotels became a home away from home with TJ, especially on Fridays. During my daily drop off from school, TJ would chat it up with my dad. He loved my dad, and I believe he was quite fond of him. He started asking, "You think your dad is up?" when he would drop me off. My dad worked nights, so he slept a few hours at a time during the day. I noticed he stayed awake when I got home so he and TJ could chat. They would talk for what seemed like forever. TJ was confident, organized, and easy to talk to. If you could get past the fact that he might fuck you up if you said the wrong thing or messed with one of "his people," he would be an awesome person. He planned everything, and I mean everything from dinner to intimacy. If he said he would be somewhere at a certain time, you could set your watch to his prompt arrival. This might sound like a desirable characteristic if I were his employer or his probation officer, but it was too much for a young woman in her first year of college. No spontaneity ever. It also came off as a little possessive. I was on the verge of spreading my wings and finding myself. This was a time when my parents lifted their rules and control, so I was not interested in trading parental guidance for partner guidance. Things turned so stale for me in my relationship with TJ that I started avoiding him at all costs.

One Friday night, TJ had made his normal movie and dinner plans. At first, I agreed, but then I decided that I had no interest in his plans for the evening. But instead of calling him and canceling the date, I avoided his calls in hopes he would get the picture. Unfortunately for me, he did not. When the time came for him to pick me up, he stopped by my parents' house and then headed over to Tai's. Once Tai told him I was not there, he would go home and try calling me later or the following day. I asked Tai to tell him she had not seen me either. Knowing he would not accept that answer, I made myself unavailable and walked up the street to wait it out over at my friend Stan's house while I left Tai to fight my battle. Little did I know that Gerald (a friend of TJ who Tai saw off and on) was going to be with him. Poor Tai. She told me they pounded her with questions, constantly called my phone, and role-played scenarios about my fate if I was with someone else. When Tai called to let me know she had calmed them down, I agreed to face the music. However, I may have created another issue. The friends whose house I was at had become increasingly uneasy about my situation and wanted to take me to the house themselves.

Not taking no for an answer, Darwin, Stan's older brother, came with me. I took a deep breath and began the walk back to Tai's. Tai came outside to update me and assure Darwin that everything was cool. He still hung around to verify that himself. As I walked through the door, Gerald came charging at me and encouraging TJ to let me have it. TJ was only one step behind him, demanding answers as well. I saw the anger on his face, but he decided to remain calm and suggested that we discuss things over dinner. Wow! After all of that, he still got his date.

It took hours to get to a destination because he was livid and wanted answers. Finally, after grabbing something to eat, he was better, but I wasn't because I knew what was coming next. I just wanted to hang out with my girlfriend, chew on snacks, and laugh, not be tied to this routine and relationship I never wanted to begin with.

During our short-lived relationship, TJ confessed his love for me. One night, before getting off the phone, I replied that I loved him too. It was word vomit. I had feelings for TJ, but not like that.

A few days after the hiding fiasco, TJ phoned me to chat, and the conversation took a chilling turn when out of nowhere, he told/warned me that he loved me so much that he couldn't handle finding out I was messing around with another guy. His exact words were, "I would have to kill that nigga and you." Both ends of the phone went silent. I thought about the movies I had seen before and reports I had heard of possessive men turning violent. I knew it was time to end this relationship, and fast. "I don't think we need to be so dramatic," I said as I thought about my relationship with Mick and another man I saw behind his back. The very next day, I rode home from school with someone else. I called TJ in advance and promised to call him later that evening. When I did, without feelings, hesitation, or beating around the bush, I went straight for the jugular and just broke it off with him. My exact words were, "I'm way too young for something serious."

Of course, I wanted him to be happy, but I needed to be happy too. And our relationship was anything but. I ignored his sobs as he brought up the fact that I said I loved him. Not to prolong this breakup, I told him I was polite and naïve when I misled him into believing I loved him after such a short time. I wished him well and promised to keep in touch, but I knew I wouldn't. Unbeknownst to the world, I was pregnant, and I was sure it wasn't his. So rather than wait around and risk it, I got the hell out of there before the shit hit the fan.

I practiced safe sex... until I didn't. When I first confirmed I was pregnant, I never considered that it might be TJ's. Against my better judgment, I selected the guy with the most money as the father, Mick. I was like a trapeze artist, swinging from one dangerous situation to the next. The other candidate was Edwin, whom I met at Forest Park community college. It was not hard to fall for the then baseball player with swag, clean cut, and a pretty smile. Edwin had the potential to go pro. We were never an official couple, but we enjoyed each other's company. Like many before, he had a friend that Tai found compatible, so double dates became our weekend thing.

I probably would have been better off if it was TJ's child. The guy, I figured as the father, Mick Wallace, was confident from the beginning that the child was not his. I told him that we could take a DNA test after delivery unless we could do it sooner. I also told Edwin the same thing. Although I had been pregnant before, this one was particularly hard. I was sick as hell from the beginning. I told Mick I wanted to end the pregnancy, and he agreed. I wanted to get the procedure done ASAP so I could feel normal again. But Mick was stalling and acting like he did not have the money. He even asked me to hold some drugs for him for about a week. He claimed he had some running around to do and would give me the money once he picked up his stuff. "Okay, whatever."

By this time, I was in no mood for formalities. I couldn't keep anything down; every smell made me nauseous, and all I could do after work or school was sleep. I was about seven weeks pregnant;

I couldn't make it one more. I was pissed about Mick's request but was too sick to protest. Not to mention how disrespectful it was to ask me to hold drugs for his ass and how disrespectful I was to my family for agreeing to do so. A week came and went with no word from Mick. I went by his house, but he wasn't there; I called, and he would give me some whack excuse. I grew sicker by the day and just wanted my life back without nausea and tiredness. So, I took matters into my own hands. Amid it all, I figured out how to pay for my abortion.

I called a couple of close friends who knew how to break down and distribute cocaine. I told them what I had and asked them to rock it and sell it so I could handle my business. Part of this arrangement gave them about a third of the profit of the original product, which was about 21 grams or a third of an ounce of cocaine. Disclaimer: My guys did ask whose product it was, if I had the right to give it away, etc. I assured them we would win if they did everything according to plan. The bad news is, in any industry, some people are very successful (like Mick), and some just get by (like my friends). It could not have been six hours from the time I gave my boys the drugs until the sound of my doorbell ringing with Mick on the other side. And, of course, after asking how I was feeling, the next thing out of his mouth was, "Can you go bring me that? My partner here is about to make a run and needs it." *Shit! What do I do now?* The mankiller would go ballistic after he found out most of it was gone. Not only was it gone, but I had given it to another man and promised him a percentage. I stood there speechless for a moment, trying to come up with a reason that would keep all hell from breaking loose.

After a moment, I decided to tell the truth. He was livid! He paused for a moment to regroup and check his hearing. I had to repeat myself twice for him to let it all sink in. I did not realize until much later that this was the single most gangster thing I had ever done. Here I was, telling an "alleged' murderer and known gang member that I had given his drugs to a couple of my male friends to sell. They were instructed to bring back all the money; I would give them a third of the profit and take care of my business with the rest. Boss move or idiot move? It did not matter; shit had gotten real and real fast. I'm from Saint Louis, a city with a high crime rate, but I think this would have gotten someone living in Idaho eliminated. Here my risk-taking ass was on my parents' porch saying that I stole product from him and gave it to another man to sell so I could use some of the proceeds to pay for an abortion of a child he wasn't even sure was his.

It was those times when I realized the Lord was watching over me. After hearing me repeat the scenario, he asked me a few questions, followed by requests. "Who did you give it to?" "When?" and finally, "Where do these niggas live?" I avoided giving too much information, and eventually, he said, "Fuck it, call 'em." I called Chris and told him what was happening, hoping he had been too busy to tamper with the drugs. Through his silence and sighs, I felt I was too late to undo what was already in the works. I asked him to bring me what he had, and how much was left uncut—(I meant not diluted with baking soda or other ingredients used to rock or crack cocaine). Mick had a nice streak and insisted that if he retrieved most of his shit untouched, there would be no harm or repercussions to the guys.

As for me, the jury was still out. No such luck today; Chris had compromised every gram of cocaine. However, he was not going to be put in a situation where he was looking over his shoulder or running for his life over a misunderstanding. He and some other friends drove to my parents' house to make a face-to-face deal with Mick. On my parents' front porch, with my family sitting less than 50 feet away inside, Mick informed Chris of his debt and gave him a certain time to repay it. As for me, once the guys left and Mick's friend went back to the car, Mick turned to me ever so politely and said these words: "Mark my words, I'm going to fuck you up for this; who do you think you are fucking with my shit? Just wait and see; you just fucked with the wrong man." With that, he turned and left. Until then, I was never scared of dying or being killed. Being pregnant was a death sentence for me. Death to my independence, my freedom, and the identity I wanted for myself. But I felt ill as I thought about someone hurting my family. I called Chris and the guys to apologize and make amends. Then I went to my room to relive it all. I stayed up all night. I ensured my mom fell asleep in the bedroom instead of in the chair or on the couch like she usually did. I remember holding my breath every time a car passed, thinking, *this is it.*

I got very little rest over the following days. You may think I was overacting, but my cousin's home was firebombed a year earlier. Her younger brother was affiliated with the Bloods (a notorious gang), and some kids, yes kids (middle school), from a rival gang threw a makeshift bomb through their front window. Their entire home was destroyed. Thank God no one was home at the time. But the thought of an entire family being displaced because of some disagreement one of its members had with a random person was frightening. As I reflected on the best and worst-case scenarios, I must have drifted off because my alarm woke me. Everything was intact, and I was still breathing. I wasn't sure if I was in the clear, but at least we made it through the night. The gunshots or firebomb never came.

SPECIAL DELIVERIES

I had difficulty convincing the two paternal candidates to take a DNA test. My goal was to eliminate whoever was not my child's father and have the one who was make a decision about being involved. Whether or not he wanted to be a part of my child's life was up to him. At the bare minimum, I could put his name on the birth certificate, and my child would have a name to start with. *For the records, my daughter was in her teens before a DNA test was administered.* Still pregnant, I continued, went to school, tried to hide the pregnancy from my parents, and worked as many hours as my body would allow. I was sick the entire time. I never went out, and I could only sleep and listen to music while lying in bed. One evening, my dad came into my room while I was taking one of my many naps. He asked me to join him in the dining room to watch TV, he asked me to call Tai, hang out, sit on the porch, or do anything else. His real request was buried in those suggestions. He wanted to believe that I had not gone and gotten pregnant again. My parents knew I was pregnant but chose to stay in denial for as long as possible. I finally emerged from my room and plopped down on the sofa. That was as far as I could get. Nausea and vomiting had taken over my life. I could not go to the hair salon, mall, or most restaurants. Everything had a smell, and those smells made me barf. It wasn't until my seventh month that I could get up and perform with some energy.

During my last trimester, a few fresh faces appeared on campus. One of them was handsome and flirtatious. I knew this was the last thing I needed, seeing that I was about to become a teenage mother. But it's not like I couldn't have friends, right? Although my stomach protruded, it did not stop the cutie from pursuing me. I would just laugh and say, "Wait! Can't you see I'm a little busy right now?" pointing to my stomach. His comment had something to do with pregnancy being desirable. "That's creepy," was my reply, and I kept it moving. As my due date approached, this dude diligently got my attention and time. We exchanged information before I left for a semester to have my baby. "I'm reaching out after you deliver," he said. I thought to myself, *this negro is crazy*. But so was I.

"Oh my God! There is so much blood; what's happening?" I asked the nurse as she attempted to lift me out of my recovery bed into a nearby wheelchair. There was so much blood that I had bled down the side of the bed, where a puddle had formed. The stupid nurse told me to keep the pressure on my uterus while bleeding. She rolled me down the hall and into my room. My mom was waiting, and my friends were on the way. As soon as I got settled, I started feeling contraction-like pains again. "Am I having twins?" I looked at my mom for answers, but she was of no help, as she looked more nervous than me. The pain intensified, and we pressed the button for nurse assistance, but no one answered. I pressed the button again … no answer. My mom had to run and grab a couple of nurses. By the time the nurses arrived, I bled through the new mattress. My cousin Dawn who also worked at the hospital, ran to get the doctor, and before I knew it, I was being transferred from my bed to another one. Then I was rushed down the hall into emergency surgery. It became painfully obvious that I was dealing with a group of dumb asses. My bed was too wide to fit through the door when I got to the operating room. The stupid nurse kept pushing and hitting the bed against the door frame as I fought back tears and screams. Finally, I decided that if I left it up to them, I would die before any procedure could be performed. I managed to say, "Wait! I'll walk in the fucking room."

Bleeding and weak, I got off the bed and walked into the

operating room for emergency surgery. Once on the table, some random ass person pried my legs open and started removing my stitches. No warning, no introduction, no information, just pulling and tugging on my sore and tender vagina. The sudden pain made me forget about the labor cramps I was having. I was dizzy. "What's wrong? Am I okay?" No one would answer my questions. Instead, some heavy women began pressing on my stomach; the sudden added pain made me scream in horror. This freak show went on for what seemed like 10 minutes or so.

Minutes later, I felt the happy serum's heavenly rush ease my body's tension. I lay there half-conscious, still asking questions while dozing off to sleep. I have no idea how I got back into my room, but I overheard my mom and doctor talking. I was hemorrhaging because of the placenta left inside my uterus during delivery. She talked as if this happened all the time, but I saw the panic in their eyes and heard the whispers of confusion and fear. In a nutshell, someone had fucked up. After everything was said and done, I had a beautiful 6 lbs. 9 oz. baby girl.

I remember the first time I held Jaimee in my arms. It was later that evening, after all the excitement of me almost bleeding to death. I was sitting in the mother's chair, gazing at this beautiful baby that had turned my life upside down. She was so little and innocent. I thought, *what am I supposed to do now?* She was perfect, and I did not want to mess her up. Maybe she could feel me staring down at her or the sadness I felt as I started to weep as she stared back at me; her facial expression seemed to say, "We'll do just fine." Then she closed her eyes and fell asleep. And for a moment, I accepted my role as her mom. As I dosed off, I thought maybe Jaimee had a purpose on this earth greater than the inconvenience that being a teenage mother brought. Then I got into bed and slept.

The thing about genes is they are passed on from one generation to the next. When my daughter was born, the questions about who the father was, was answered. She strongly resembled Edwin. Thick eyebrows, big, beautiful eyes, and a wide nose. Yet I still left open the possibility that she could be Mick's child because looks can be deceiving. Years passed, and neither Mick nor Edwin stepped up to be tested or provide for Jaimee. Mick and I later reconciled, and he half-heartedly came to see her when she was around two weeks old and again when she was three.

Regardless of those losers, my child was well taken care of. She was the apple of my parents' eyes. My dad would always have her in his arms, buy her whatever she wanted, read to her, everything. Since she was the first granny baby to hail from the house on Ferguson Ave, she was smothered with attention. Jaime was mature for her age and enjoyed watching educational shows and learning new things. She was always around adults and liked it that way for a brief period. Kids were weird to her. She would stare or get frustrated if they got too close. It was hilarious to watch, but that is how she was. She figured she was the only little one in this world and did not need anyone else to compete with.

That changed when she started attending daycare. She had no choice but to loosen up; it took a while, but she eventually became a gregarious person. It also helped that the daycare she attended was at Tai's mom's house, "gran gran" is what Jaimee called her. She ran an in-home daycare, and between her curriculum and my parents' involvement and patience, Jaimee had an environment that fostered learning. I took care of my baby, played with her, and took her everywhere, but I was still me. Wild and searching. The lifestyle I managed as a parent soon saw me at odds with my dad. He was unhappy about Jaimee always being on the road with me or being watched by other people. I never thought I was disrespecting my parents by always taking Jaimee with me. I thought I was doing what I was supposed to do. But I was spending a lot of nights at Tai's because it was convenient and fun. I took on and handled my responsibilities both with Jaimee and within my parents' home. But a storm was on the horizon, and I was none the wiser.

One afternoon, I stopped by the house to gather more clothes for several days. My dad took that time to communicate his feelings about the time Jaimee and I were gone. He was pissed that all I did was stop by to get clothes, so he said to me, and I quote, "Why don't you just move your ass in with your friends?" I replied in true Ellison fashion, "Okay." I saw the hurt on his face as soon as I said it. The joy that had come into his life was being kept away from him because his selfish and immature daughter and her wayward ways. I wish I could have changed my reaction, but I was a young lady with a hard head and a point to prove. I was not exactly sure what that point was, but I stayed away for six months. I would visit, and Jaimee stayed with my parents from time to time, but it wasn't the same.

My dad called Tai's house a few days before Christmas to speak to me. He asked me if we were spending Christmas with Tai's family. I heard the sadness in his voice, and it was then that I realized my dad was asking us to come home. I never wanted to leave in the first place. I just had a little more flexibility at Tai's house than at home. I packed our stuff, cleaned our space, and returned to my father's house. My dad and I never spoke about it again. We were back, and that is all that mattered ... to both of us. I missed my home just as much as my parents and brothers. And to Tai, Ms. Gia, Aunt Catherine, Tabatha, and Trac. I love you all for always treating us as one of your own.

My cup runneth over as I entered corporate America. I had to be accountable to both my job and my kid, without missing a beat in my social life. And happy hour was the perfect solution to mitigate a work-life balance crisis. On Fridays, after I picked Jaime up from school and grabbed us something to eat, I would drop her off at my parents' house and head back out. One Friday, my friends and I were at our usual happy hour spot, (Hadley's), and in walked Edwin. By this time, I had not seen or heard from him in almost four years. As soon as he saw me, he walked over, hugged me, and asked, "Where is my daughter?' Although a bar is not the ideal place to talk about paternity and kids, I took the opportunity to bring him up to speed on all things regarding Jaimee. I was out with Cali, who lived up the street from the bar, so she volunteered to go home and grab all the photos she had of Jaimee (this was before cell phones had a camera). When Cali returned with the photos, he looked them over like a proud father and said, "I don't have to look at the pictures to know she's mine." *Really? Then why haven't you met her, called, or checked on her?* I thought this to myself because no answer he gave would have made a difference. Edwin's comments made me want to punch him in the face. *Because it sounds like you purposely abandoned your responsibilities,* I further thought *we don't even know much about each other. I could have been an abusive person or just an overall piece of shit-ass mom while you sat here and confirm your relationship with a child you have never met.* The more I thought about it, the better off I felt Jaimee was without his influence. At first, I thought crossing each other's paths was divine intervention, and my daughter would finally meet her father. But despite his proclamation of fatherhood, it would be almost twelve years from that encounter before the two would speak and another year before they would meet.

Kids need both of their parents, or else the creator would have allowed us to reproduce without each other. It was no sweat off my back, though, because Jaimee had a village that loved and supported her. However, the village could not fill the void of a father. Even as a small child, she would ask about her dad. Sometimes she would make remarks like, "Mom! I think I saw my daddy today," or, "What did you say my dad's name is?" or, "Do you know where my dad lives?" Since no one had stepped up to take a DNA test, I continued to tell Jaime that her dad was Mick. She had a name; all she needed was a face to put with it.

One evening, while helping the girls with their homework, Tai called. She had bumped into Edwin at a local store and given him my phone number. I was excited because I wanted my daughter to get the needed answers. The bad thing about this exchange is that Edwin failed to give Tai his number, and it would be another year before the opportunity presented itself again. He never called. I kept this information to myself, waiting on the day the phone would ring and Edwin would be on the other end looking to start a relationship with someone he believed to be his daughter. He was a joke. Shameless. A year later, Tai called with similar news, she had bumped into Edwin yet again; this time, she got *his* number and called me with it while he was standing there. We spoke briefly and arranged for Edwin to call Jaimee on her sixteenth birthday (a week later).

On the morning of her sixteenth birthday, I asked Jaimee if she would dial the number that I placed inside her birthday card. She looked puzzled but anxious at the same time. "Whose number is this?" she asked.

"You'll find out when you call," was my response. Laila glanced over at me, searching for clues, but this was Jaimee's moment. Sixteen years in the making. Jaimee dialed the number. "Hello. This is Jaimee Ellison, I was told to call this number." After a few seconds, she was smiling from ear to ear.

I decided I could spill the beans to Laila. "Oh! I'm so happy for her. Followed by, "Where has he been?" The look on both of their faces was priceless for very different reasons.

"Nearly all men can stand adversity, but if you want to test a man's character, give him power." Abraham Lincoln

NAÏVE OR STUPID

Remember the dude I exchanged numbers with before I left school to go on maternity leave? His name is Owen. Owen would be the man who single-handedly made me lose my mind and my way. In business school, we are taught to perform a SWOT analysis for business. The SWOT analysis is an acronym for strengths, weaknesses, opportunities, and threats. It helps businesses decide how to enter a market, positioning, or rather or not to pursue the venture at all. It makes perfectly good sense. Why spend all your time, resources, talent, and creativity without initial market research to confirm or debunk a product or service's value in that market. Which leads me to my next point … we should probably apply this same logic before entering a relationship. Although it would not be as spontaneous and fun as winging it, it would save us a lot of wasted time, energy, disappointment, and heartbreak. The good thing about performing this analysis is even if the results are unfavorable, you can still proceed with a better understanding of what to expect. The downside is that people are not as easy to monitor as the spending habits of coffee drinkers or the purchasing patterns of new moms. People, by their very definition, are unpredictable.

Nevertheless, I vowed to experiment with this going forward before getting into bed—literally or figuratively—with someone new. Sometimes I listened to the results, and sometimes, I ignored them. So, against all the gut instincts in the world, I proceeded to participate in relationships with partners that racked up considerably more points in the weakness and threat categories than the strength and opportunity ones. Maybe I should have performed a SWOT analysis on myself.

Owen and I started great, but the saying "it's not how you start but how you finish" had that relationship in mind. In the beginning, Owen was kind, considerate, and very generous with his time and money; I couldn't have been happier. Physically, he was my type, He had beautiful teeth, clear skin, was over six feet tall, and if you put a watch on his cock, it would look like an arm. Those were his physical attributes. The things he wanted me to see. Yet it would be the things that were not so visible that would break me as a woman.

We became an item around the time Jaimee was six months old. When I wasn't in school or working, most likely, we were together, Jaimee in tow. Owen came from a large family, so it was always something to do or someone to hang with. His siblings consisted of two brothers (one older and one younger) and two sisters (both younger). He also had a slew of uncles from their mid-twenties through his early thirties. Age was just a number, and we all had something in common at this point in our lives. We liked to party. One evening, a group of us went to a popular East Saint Louis club called The Maxx. It was one of the hot spots "across the water" (the Mississippi River) East Saint Louis is in Illinois; that is why we say across the water because you must cross the Mississippi River Bridge to get there. The night was off to a good start, and we were drinking, dancing, and having a great time when suddenly, I saw Owen's oldest daughter's mother flirting with him. Now, it is quite possible that she was just being cordial because they shared a daughter. But my drunken mind interpreted the interaction as disrespect. I was a jealous type of person, so this did not sit well with me. When confronted, he said she was just speaking to him about their child, and I had nothing to worry about. In somebody's else life, that would have been the end of it, but not for me. Not that she owed me anything, but her rudeness was unnecessary, and it reminded me of how

Cassie used to behave when she was part of my past love triangle. And we know how that turned out.

When leaving, Owen rode home with me, and his brother and Tai drove his car. When we pulled up to his place around 1:45 a.m., a set of headlights hit my rearview mirror as we parked. To my dismay, it was her ... his child's mother. The alcohol consumption from the night was making me increasingly irritable. Finally, I jumped out of the car to confront her about coming to his house this late, to which she said, "Owen told me to come."

I replied, "Really? He told you to follow *us*? Are we having a threesome or something?" She was a smart-mouthed little heifer, and I would have loved nothing more than to hit her with my car ... twice. Owen admitted he asked her to follow us so he could give t her some money she had asked for earlier. He did not have it on him, so he asked her to follow us to his house. "This couldn't wait until tomorrow?" I asked. Then an argument ensued. Back and forth, she and I went. When she finally sped off, the argument continued between Owen and me. As our voices grew louder, he reached out and slapped me. I was stunned. *Who does this punk think he is? Screw this; I'm out.* I grabbed my keys, told Tai to get in my car, and sped off. That was the end of the relationship. Well, that is how it should have happened. His constant calls of apology and regret over his behavior got him back in my graces. Stupid, right? The worst thing is I cannot blame him fully. I allowed this behavior to exist in our relationship by taking him back. It's like blaming a clown for being a clown instead of taking some accountability for my going to the circus. I can't put a sound explanation of why I stayed, but I did. At best, I was a silly drunken child playing a game where the stakes involved real people and consequences that lasted a lot longer than the relationship.

Throughout our turbulent, on-and-off situation, we traveled, laughed, shared tears, raised kids, attended weddings, buried friends, celebrated birthdays, and inflected the type of pain on each other that would give Stephen King a concept for his best horror story to date. Owen met a broken, hurt, lonely, alcoholic teenager on the verge of becoming a mother to her first child. I met a disappointed young father who wanted to change the direction his life was headed by doing what he always did. Regardless of our backgrounds, we were both on the wrong path. Too young to understand how we were the authors of our own stories, too discombobulated to do something about it if we did. The two of us together were fire and gasoline. Explosive. There were good times, for we got along great when alcohol was not involved. When we drank, which was all the time, we did not. I continued my studies and completed my associate degree while he hustled and tried to appease the many people who needed something from him. We partied, worked hard, and navigated through life as a couple... or so I thought.

I sometimes hung out with his sister Mia. She, Tai, and I would hit the club from time to time. Coming back from hanging out one night, I was dropping Mia off at home, and as we pulled up to her place, she candidly said, "Faye, I can't do this no more; you are too good to my brother for him to be doing what he is doing." My heart stopped, just like it did when I pulled up at Cassie's house and saw Galvin on her porch. She told me all about Owen's escapades with a woman named Lola. He had brought her to their house, and everyone had met her, and they had all hung out and on and on. Mia told me I needed to confront him, and if I needed Lola's information for verification, she would be happy to help. She added, "One last thing, don't let Owen know I told you," She got out of the car and disappeared into the house.

I sat in silence for about 10 minutes. I was mad, hurt, and sad all at once. I was so emotional that I felt my body shaking. When Galvin cheated in high school, I was smarter and knew it was time to move on. I was too young to fight for anybody at that point, but here I was five years later, dealing with the same shit. Part of me wanted to say nothing and never speak to him again. But the loudest part of me wanted answers and to hear his side. It was as if someone had turned the volume down on the universe, and all that was left was the heavy beating of my heart. Tears of anger and sadness rolled down my cheeks. I started my car and proceeded home. I wanted to hop on the highway and disappear from it all. But life doesn't quite work that way. I would have to have a conversation with the man I considered my friend and lover about the state of our relationship ... again. I confronted Owen a couple of days later. He won by denying everything.

He claimed they had a mutual friend, which is why Lola would sometimes be at his house. She would stop by the house asking for him. He had made it clear that he was in a relationship and showed her no interest. So, I stayed yet again, against and better judgment. It only got worse. On one of our many nights out partying, Tai and I started at a popular nightclub called *Mirage*. Owen and I agreed to meet later at another club across the water at a spot called *The Terrace*. Both clubs were packed as usual. When we arrived at the nightclub later that night, we scoped out the place for a minute, then headed to an upstairs bar. At the bar, we bumped into an old classmate from high school. He offered me another drink, and we started a friendly conversation. Out of the blue, Owen appeared; he began arguing with me about flirting with people in his presence. Before I could open my mouth to make the introductions, he cursed, waved me off, and stormed away from the bar. A little more than ~~drunk~~ tipsy at this point, I excused myself to speak with him in private (if I could catch up with him). It was a strange reaction to absolutely nothing. I mean, after all, people socialize in clubs, right? With his attitude and unwillingness to talk to me, I became agitated.

Once we reached the main level, he headed to one of the bars with me closely behind. I planted myself before him as he steered me to his left side. I heard a female ask, "Owen, who the fuck is this?" "This" meaning me. The vigor in her voice let me know she was not a friend or someone he had just met. Instead, this woman spoke with the same confusion as any woman who was being duped.

I was like, "I'm Faye, his woman," pointing at Owen.

She smiled condescendingly. "Oh, so you're Faye?" He told me about you." Then she pushes him in the face, yelling, "I thought you said you'd broken up!" Owen's dumbfounded look just made things escalate. When he did not respond like she believed he should have, she smacked him square in the face again. So, I balled my fist and gave him some solid punches too. No need to let her have all the fun. Owen pushed her back, and security yanked us out of the club before any more hits were exchanged. Wow! One minute I'm sipping on a drink, enjoying conversation and music, and the next, I'm being introduced to the other side of my love triangle. Her name was Lola, and I had no idea what he could have seen in her. Basic as beige paint.

After being thrown out of the club, the three of us ended up in the alley next to it. Here we were in one of the most dangerous cities in America, drunk, pissed, and enraged. Owen was still going back and forth, trying to convince Lola and me that this was all a misunderstanding, but I knew better. This was the woman Owen's sister confided to me about earlier that month. I remained quiet as Lola disclosed the details of their relationship through her screams and profanity. Owen was grabbing her and talking over her. Finally, she yelled, "I'll be right back," and headed back towards the club.

Alone in the alley with this fool, "She drunk, babe," was his excuse for all that had just happened.

Although intoxicated, I was just sober enough to be quick on my feet. I cut him off, "If that's who you want to be with, fuck it. I can have another you by *tomorrow*—" Before the last couple of letters from the word tomorrow could leave my lips, I felt my unsteady body hit the uneven brick-laid ground. To soften the impact, I landed on my hands and knees. Trying to pull myself up from the pavement, I was struck again by the man who once promised that he would kill me if *I* tried to leave. Maybe he was a man of his word. His kicking and punching a drunken woman in stilettos made me believe he was carrying out his promise.

As voices started to fill the alley, he stopped hitting me and helped me up as if I had been attacked by someone other than him. He mumbled under his breath, "Straighten up; you alright." I snatched away and started towards my car. Word about our foolishness must have spread throughout the club, as more people assembled outside. I was looking for Tai so we could leave. All the while, Owen was pushing me back toward his car. I asked if he could just find Tai and have her come out so I could go home. She had my car keys, and I wanted nothing more than to get out of there. I was angry, hurt, bleeding, and sick. Owen picked me up and carried me to his car that his brother had pulled around front. I sat in the backseat assessing the damage to my wrist, feet, and torn, bloodstained clothes. My hair was all over the place, my shirt and suede vest had blood on them, the thumb of my freshly done acrylic nails was broken, my knee-highs were holding on by a thread around my ankles, and my wrist was bleeding from the glass embedded in them from the fall.

"What the F... is going on?" Aggressive voices came from behind as they approached the car. It was Lola, and she had returned with backup. I thought to myself, *Great, what a perfect way to end the evening, getting my ass kicked by a bunch of drunken women over a man who couldn't keep his dick in his pants.* I secretly hoped for the best, I figured I probably would not feel anything at this point, but if it was going down, I wanted to start on my feet. I slowly exited the car and stood my ground as they formed a semi-circle around us.

A little background on Lola. She was allegedly part of a girl gang called the Switchblade Sisters. Their mission was to leave physical markings on their opponent with a switchblade, usually on the face. I heard a story about a very attractive young lady who came to blows with Lola over another man and is now living with a daily reminder of their run-in on her cheek. I was too drunk to fear that fate even though it crossed my mind.

Thank God for grace; Lola and her crew were chill about the fiasco. It seemed like they were more interested in the reason behind the brawl than throwing fuel on the flames. I guess Lola figured, *What the hell ... we both got played.* It became apparent that Owen wasn't comfortable having an open dialogue with the two women he was dating simultaneously. As Lola started to yell out more details of his affairs, he snatched her out of the group and dragged her towards the lower steps. I was more distracted by her crew's proximity to me than anything else. A few of them ran over to pull Owen off Lola; he had succeeded in getting her to the lower lot. Then I heard a loud crashing sound. Owen had picked Lola up and slammed her down on top of someones' car hood. Her backup was in full pursuit, and I was off the hook. His brother grabbed my arm and led me back to his car, then went to retrieve Owen before he caught a case. Tai emerged from the club, looking dazed, confused, and wanting answers. Hell!

So, did I. Where were the police? Security? Concerned citizens? I had gotten beaten in public by a man who was now fighting another woman, and besides his brother, no help came. I understood we were in East Saint Louis, but this was ridiculous.

I felt that familiar pain of being discarded and used. The same pain I first felt all those years ago when my cousin sodomized me, the same pain when my granny failed to take me to the hospital after I broke my nose. I could feel my walls of defense rising higher.

By the time we got to his house, I was exhausted, and for a good reason. The ordeal went on forever. I must have blacked out or something because there is no way I could have tolerated that bull crap for such an extended period. Shortly after getting to his place, all hell broke loose again. I had my second wind and had had enough. I grabbed a broom and swung at Owen. Then I charged him as hard as possible, and we both went down onto the kitchen floor. I tried to cut off his air supply by pressing the broom handle against his throat. While he defended himself and struggled to throw me off the top of him, Owen swung at me and landed a punch directly on my right eye. I grabbed my eye in horror. At first, I thought he scratched me under my eye because I could feel the burning sensation of a fresh cut. However, his reaction told me something different. He got up, started rummaging through the freezer and drawers, and assembled a makeshift ice pack. He got me to calm down and administered ice to my eye. It was daylight out, and I was exhausted. I demanded that he call me a taxi, then passed out.

I woke up about four hours later to a pounding headache, a tender ankle, and what I thought was the swelling from a scratch under my right eye. Tai had driven herself home, and Owen's car was not there either. He called his brother to come to take me home, but I called a taxi instead. When it arrived, I got in and gave the man my address. I received a weird and puzzled look from the driver, but I blew it off. I knew I was a sight for sore eyes with my bloodstained clothes and uncombed hair. I sat back and tried not to replay the events of the previous evening in my pounding head, and then I saw it. In the rearview mirror sitting behind the taxi driver, a young woman who slightly resembled me but with a right eye almost swollen shut. I was so startled I turned around to see if someone else was behind me. I felt the tension in my chest as I mentally scrambled for an excuse to give my parents. Surely there would be questions as their daughter walked into the house looking as if she had gone a couple of rounds with Mike Tyson. I understood the look on the driver's face. Shit! I had to go to work and school the following day as well. It was going to be a long week. How in the world was I going to play this off? The answer came as quickly as the night before had escalated… I was not. At that point, I did not owe anyone an explanation except my parents. In the meantime, I would deal with the stares from my professors, classmates, co-workers, and onlookers. As I approached the front door to my parents' house, I took a deep breath and let myself in.

Jaimee must have heard me coming through the door because she was waiting on the other side when I opened it. Fat cheeks and adorableness greeted me, but when she saw my face, she let out a small scream and ran towards the kitchen. My dad did a slight double-take but managed to keep quiet as my mom walked into the living room and gave a gasp. I did not know what to say, so I lowered my head and went to my room, with my mom and Jaimee close behind. Once in the room, my mom asked quietly, "Fatou, what happened?" Jaimee was peeking from behind her, squinting as if she, too, was examining me. I told my mom that I had had a run-in with some girls, and the group of them got the best of me. I am unsure if she bought my story, but I knew my dad did not. I could feel how tense he was and knew what he was thinking. I would never have admitted it; if I had, that would have meant the end of my communication with Owen, and I was not quite ready for that.

In the days following "the incident," Owen called a lot. But what do you say to someone who kicked your ass in front of the entire world? Things got awkward for about a week. I went about my life, work, family, school, and my new bluish-black eye. I never tried to hide it; when people asked me if I were okay, I would just say, "Besides my right eye, yes." It took a little over a week for all the swelling to go down and a couple more for the discoloration to fade. I was bruised but feeling better. A month before the smackdown, Owen and the rest of the crew had purchased concert tickets to see LSG and Missy Elliott. Thankfully, Mia came in his place. I masked the trauma of the public fight and got dolled up for the first time in weeks to go to the concert. It was so amazing. For the few hours we spent singing, dancing, and screaming, I forgot about all that had transpired. A couple of songs performed by LSG made me reflect on the state of my life and relationship, almost bringing me to tears, but I shook it off, ordered another cocktail, and sang harder than Johnny Gill himself. After the concert, Owen called to ask if I could speak with him when I dropped Mia off. The time we spent away from each other lifted a weight I did not know existed. After all he owed me an apology, for everything, and I owed myself one for losing myself in that relationship.

It would take years of therapy and working on myself to understand that I was not attracted to him. I was attracted to the access to my true first love ... alcohol, for which I had an unquenchable thirst. My choice of men would continue to resemble a pattern until I came to terms with what battle I was fighting. I was an addict, and they were my pusher. I had turned my disappointments, loneliness, and anger into an insatiable drinking problem. More than the money, more than the sex, more than love itself, I gave more time to the man with an open schedule over the one taking night classes, keeping his credit in check, and building wealth. I wanted what the latter man offered but with the first guy's flexibility. Not likely; thus, the reason I had a string of bullshit relationships full of neediness and missed opportunities for true love. From the ages of 19 to 23, I drank more than I slept, and because of that, all the hard work (mother, employee, colleague, student, member) was all but void because I was always distracted by the need to drink. I completed all my duties and took care of my responsibilities, but having a cocktail was always the end game. I guess getting punched and kicked in public provided clarity but not sobriety.

During this time, my high school beau, Galvin, reached out. He had joined the military and was stationed in California, where he and Cassie lived in matrimony. Late one night, while everyone in my house slept, I was awakened by the sound of our house phone ringing. It took me a second to realize no one else would pick it up, so I speed-walked to the living room to answer it. "May I speak to Faye?" the caller said.

"This is she; who's calling?" was my reply.

"Hey, this is Galvin." This was before caller ID, but I knew who it was before I asked.

He went on to say how he was just thinking about me and heard I had a daughter and was seeing someone. I just listened. He wanted to see how I was doing and to say hi. I did not have much to say but thanked him for thinking of me. And that was that. He sounded like a man who was living the life of his choices. Not happy, not unhappy, just living. After our short conversation, I lay in bed and pondered what life with him would have been like if we had kept our child and moved to San Francisco with him and his pro footballer player cousin. I rested well after those thoughts, knowing that it was him, not me, stuck in a relationship purgatory of his own making.

Fast forward two and a half years, and I was pregnant with my second child. I remember still being hopeful about finishing college, moving out of state, and providing a very comfortable life for my kids. As I shared my aspirations with Owen, he made a comment that I have struggled to prove him wrong since the words were spoken. "Moving?" he said, half laughing. "Where the hell are you going to go with two kids?" I was still answering that question years later. It spoke to all my fears about being a young mother. I asked him to repeat his question to ensure I heard him correctly. Because what I heard was his doubt that I could rebound from what others may take on as an excuse to stay mediocre.

I exhaled to clear my head and then I saw him for what he was at that moment. I turned to Owen and said without blinking, "Since you feel that way, let's see where the fuck you're going with five kids." He looked puzzled, as if I had started speaking Portuguese or something. "When I deliver this baby, he or she will be going home with you. Since you want another baby so bad, another baby you shall get". Furthermore, if you are not at the hospital to uphold your end of the deal, foster care will have a beautiful new baby boy or girl to add to the system." I regretted the words before I spoke them, but I knew I had to stand firm once I did. I could feel the shit storm I had just released with my declaration. Some part of me did not think I could do it, but the loudest part was egging me on to stand my ground.

With this short conversation, I had mentally set in motion a chain of events that would give way to my biggest mistake to date. During Laila's birth, Owen was a noticeable "no-show." So, true to my word, I begrudgingly signed the papers and gave my beautiful baby girl up for adoption. Laila was not immediately taken from me. She stayed in my room overnight, and I stayed awake watching her every move.

The staff at the hospital probably assumed that I would have a change of heart. And the way Laila looked at me, I felt she thought the same. She had the same look on her precious face that her sister did a few years earlier that seemed to say, "Don't worry, Mom, you got this." For a newborn, Laila took a long time to fall asleep. She just watched me as if she wanted to remember my face. My perfect baby was taken the next afternoon before I was released. There was no fanfare, no visitors, no well-wishers. My family and close friends were all aware of my plans and decided not to show their support for a decision they did not agree with.

Upon my release from the hospital, my dad waited in front of the hospital for me. The ride home was a quiet one. Once I got there, my brothers and mom were sitting at the dining room table. I gave a halfhearted "Hey" under my breath and went into my room. My family's silence was so loud that I needed to leave the house to hear my thoughts. I gathered Jaimee and some overnight clothes, then left. Feeling physically weak, I drove around for a while before finally checking into a hotel. I bathed and prepared both of us for bed.

By that time, I was ready for a permanent nap. I had given birth to two healthy, beautiful baby girls, and here I was in a hotel room, one daughter jumping around and having the time of her life and the other in the company of strangers. But I needed rest to sort things out and emerge stronger and self-assured. Jaimee was running back and forth; her little fat hands kept hitting the bed, and she kept turning the volume on the TV. You would have thought she was on the set of *Looney Tunes,* and I was on the set of *the Saddest movie ever.* At this time, my body started to react to the stress of it all. I was sweating profusely, and I suddenly had the chills.

My attempts to fall asleep were useless as I lay there in excruciating pain. It felt like I was on fire while walking naked in the middle of an ice storm. Finally, I decided to call an ambulance. When they arrived, I was too weak to open the door. The front office had to let them in. I was a little scared and a little elated. I figured if I was going to die, I no longer had to make decisions, be sad or feel alone. At 23, I had given birth to my second child by a second man and was alone and sick in a hotel room with an EMT taking my temperature and trying to keep me coherent. I was encouraged to leave with them but opted out. Instead, I was given fluids and ibuprofen and warned to see my doctor. All the excitement must have drained Jaimee because she got into bed and fell fast asleep once they left.

I woke the next day a little tired but feeling better. I figured since I made it through the night, I might as well face my issues like an adult. I ordered us something to eat, bathed, and drove back to my parents' house. My family was relieved and hopeful that a day to reflect had provided clarity. I called the hospital to find out Laila's whereabouts and arranged a meeting to get her back. The call alone brought me back to health. I still had to speak with Owen, but I felt hopeful and stronger. I needed strength to explain Owen's and my plans to my parents. I wanted them to understand that, for the time being, he would be the primary caregiver. At this juncture, I was still a little overwhelmed and unsure about my decision to have Owen take on custody. But I had to trust the process and believe things would work out for the best. I never planned on giving my daughter up for adoption, and although I was too immature to call my move strategic, it was. Parenting is nothing to take lightly, and with me on my second and Owen on his fifth, I could not risk doing it on my own again. Plus, this kind of jolt to normalcy would make us think twice about our recklessness. We both created her, and we were both going to raise her. He and I scheduled a time to meet at foster care; when we arrived, they gave us pictures of Laila and updates on the week's events. They wanted to make sure we agreed on our next move. Their main concern was for Laila; the organization that took care of her temporary placement wanted to ensure we had a plan and intended to stay the course.

When Laila was brought out for us to hold, she was more beautiful than I remembered. I felt a bolt of pride run through my veins. I could see the emotions building up in Owen as he held her tiny body. We walked into that office as young adults, but we walked out as grown-ass people. Laila had a lot of love waiting for her, and Owen and I both had a lot of support. Some people faulted me for my initial decision and said I was running away from my responsibilities. But things became less awkward after the smoke cleared, and people began to wrap their minds around a father being a primary caregiver. Years later, the same doubters started to make comments like, "A child has two parents" and "More men should step up and do what Owen did." "Girl, I don't blame you; I wish I could have let my child's father raise him/her." Once we made it look easy, everyone had different opinions. At first, I was at Owen's, or he was bringing Laila to my parents' house daily. We were focused on doing the best thing for our daughter. Things were good ... in the beginning.

THE GIRLS

My daughters brought me a lot of joy. I know I did not always show it, but they did. If I had to do it all over again, I would only change the timing. If I had to choose kids over the husband, I had always chosen the legacy…my kids. It seemed like too much work to have both at the same time. One expects a child to need guidance, nurturing, discipline, bathing, feeding, educating, and so on. What I discovered is men need almost all the same damn things. I take my hat off to women who manage all the wants and needs of spouses and children. I have concluded wives and mothers give the greatest sacrifice. Like my mom, she put her desires on hold and committed herself completely to her family. She is a bigger and better person than I ever could have been. That frustration I once had with her vanished the day I had Jaimee. I got it.

My girls are my heartbeats; they give me energy, purpose, and drive. They challenged me as no class assignment had done before. Being a mom provides an education unrivaled by the world's leading institutions. When things were good, I felt honored to have been blessed with two such amazing and spirited young beings. When things were hard, I felt sympathy for them and shame for myself. Being a mom meant juggling the endless list of roles; cook, chauffeur, doctor, psychologist, police, judge and jury, housekeeper, teacher, minister, lecturer, maid, provider, guard, nutritionist, hairstylist, seamstress, educator, punisher, banker, friend, and dad if you're single. I do not have to say this to the millions of women and men doing the same thing and maybe even more. But raising two little girls while coming of age became overwhelming at times. Not to say men do not face their challenges as parents, but since I have no experience with being male, I can only speak from my perspective. Growing up, my dad brought home the bacon, but my mom cleaned the pan, cooked it, served it, and cleared the table. At some point, I decided it was easier to raise my girls without the constant interference of a partner. My girls may have felt differently, but they had my dad, my brothers, and Owen every step of the way.

From the beginning, my youngest daughter, Laila, was a pistol. Opinionated and loved to do things her way. She would throw a tantrum if someone attempted to help her, like removing her coat or taking the wrapper off a piece of candy. she interprets it as attempted robbery, instead of the assistance being offered. Case in point, one Friday night, the girls and I Stayed at Tai's house for a movie night. Laila was almost two at the time. When we got to Tai's, she placed our bags in the guest room. Shortly after prepping our food and settling in to watch a movie, Laila started whining and searching around Tai's living room, then her kitchen, followed by a silent tantrum. We watched in bewilderment. "Laila, baby, what's wrong?" "My bag! Where is my bag?" she fussed.

"Wait! your diaper bag?"

To which she replied, "Yes! I had it, and now it's gone." Not to provoke her further, I fought back a hearty laugh from the foolishness I was hearing. Laila thinking someone stole her diaper bag was a little more than hilarious. I got up to retrieve ~~her~~ it and put her at ease. When I returned with it, you would have thought she found a lost puppy. She grabbed the bag and spent the night with it on her shoulder. Her possessions were her prizes. I'm glad she eventually grew out of this feeling of lack and became a little more giving.

Jaimee and Laila were as different as night and day. Laila's the perfect mix of both her dad and me. Although I did not see it initially, this child was a manipulator. She was wise for her age and knew what to say and not say around her parents regarding the other. She was spoiled and read people well. Her temperament for certain things was short, and she loved cleanliness and organization. She was a little hustler and a hard worker, and those attributes served her well. Laila knew she was the apple of her dad's eye and got over on him every chance she got.

When Laila's father and I decided it was time for her to live with me full-time, I was excited to have my daughter home, and I also had my doubts about the transition. Laila and her dad were connected at the hip, and the lifestyle and freedom she enjoyed with him would be quite different with me. Although he did his best, she needed guidance and structure that was missing while living with him. As the disciplinarian, I struggled with her after she spent time with him or his family. But with consistency and patience, we made it work.

Now, my firstborn, Jaimee, was as sharp as a whistle. She was attentive and had what old folks called "the been here before syndrome." Learning was easy for her, being still and quiet was easy for her, and she was overall a great baby. Just like her sister, she got along with everyone. Finding a babysitter was never a problem; sometimes, it became an all-out war over who would get an opportunity to watch Jaimee, a great problem to have, right? Jaimee was funny and mature for her age. But one funny moment stands out from the rest. It came at the hand of my dad's favorite piece of profanity…motherfucker. I have heard a lot of kids try their luck with using profanity; the younger they are, the funnier it is. Normally you hear words like shit or damn, but not my Jay.

One evening, my mom and I, along with my brothers, were sitting at the dining room table playing a board game. My dad worked nights, so he typically was asleep around 7:00 p.m. after the evening news went off unless it was Thursday, and the *Cosby Show* was on. This night was no different. We got a little rowdy playing Monopoly and started disputing each other's plays and moves. This friendly argument went on for a while. Then, out of nowhere, without even looking up from her lap, Jaimee said, "Shut up motherfuckers," after which you could feel the air leave the room as we all looked in shock and then scattered like roaches when the lights were turned on. We knew my dad would commence killing us all because Jaimee had a potty mouth.

Moments later, my dad appeared in the doorway, sleepy-eyed and dazed. He rubbed his head and said with his shoulders slumped, "That's not nice, grandbaby, don't say things like that." Then he proceeded to go through his nightly routine of getting ready for work. Jaimee knew she was in trouble when my dad came out of the room, but to her surprise, he just made that comment and went to shower. She followed him to the restroom and sat outside the door until he emerged. Her pink cotton nightgown hung to the top of her fat feet as she followed him in silence to the bedroom, the kitchen, and finally to the front door as she did most nights. She would have followed him to the car if he did not stop her. My dad nodded and said goodnight to all of us as he passed through the dining room. When he got to the front door, he picked Jaimee up and kissed her on her cheek, and said in a playful voice, "Night, night, grandbaby," as he pulled his skull cap on tight to brace for the October chill; he opened the front door letting the cold night air get past him and kiss us on the ankles. Jaimee shrugged her shoulders without missing a beat, then said, clear as day, "Night motherfucker," and laughed.

My dad shook his head and closed the door behind him. We sat at the table, mouths open, eyes bulging and frozen. But when motherfucker is your favorite curse word, you will be called one sooner or later. Probably not by your grandchild, but sooner or later. Sorry Pops! I did not know what to do, and she heard it from him first. I speed-walked to grab her foul-mouthed butt and put her to bed. I explained that she could not say words like that and that she hurt Pawpaw's feelings. She looked as if she was apologetic, turned over, and went to sleep. Once I put her to bed, my brothers and I laughed until we cried. Kids do say the darndest things.

Ever since Jaimee's birth, the occupants of 1140 had become a family again. Babies have a way of bringing happiness or newness. The daily stress of five people cohabitating was put on hold while we enjoyed watching this little person explore and grow. It had been a long time since belly laughs were a daily thing. I saw the joy in my dad's eyes for the first time in a long time. He has the most beautiful smile with deep dimples. I was privileged to see them every day now that Jaimee was in our lives. When he got off work, my room was the first place he came to, smiling and doing whatever he could to wake Jaimee up. Although I was an unwed teenage mother, Jaimee was the best thing that could have happened to 1140.

ON THE EDGE

Things started to deteriorate just as Owen, and I got into a healthy rhythm with co-parenting. No longer in a relationship, he moved in with his once side chick, now the main chick, Lola. History had repeated itself, this time with a bonus ... our daughter. I could not expect anything different from a liar and a cheat. Don't get me wrong, Owen was not the best boyfriend, but I knew he would be the opposite regarding his daughter. I also knew his moving in with Lola was more strategic than love. Laila was living with him full-time, and he needed an in-house mother figure to help him with daily tasks. True to form, he denied living with Lola, and I denied myself sanity.

On evening, Owen and I checked into a downtown hotel for the night. Around 3:00 a.m., we were awakened by his cell phone. It was Lola, and she wanted to personally deliver the news that all four of his newly purchased tires had been sliced. I guess she had her suspicions about him ending things with me. When he did not come home or call her, she set out to catch him in the act. Most liars and cheaters are creatures of habit, and he was no exception. Owen was so brazen, that he frequented the same hotel they shared when they first met. He had it like that with both of us. Collectively we had given Owen the power to fuck both of us, literally and figuratively. I may have met him while he was working on his associate degree in communication, but he already had a Ph.D. in women. He was very skilled and persuasive. I was young and overwhelmed by his looks, charisma, and charitable efforts. I had no idea that the decision to continue to be disrespected would take over a decade to repair. It took an unplanned murder-suicide to snap me out of my stupor.

I went as far as hiring a private investigator to collect some information on Owen and Lola. The investigator I contacted somehow got into Owen's car and provided me with receipts, license plate number, addresses, and car descriptions of both Owen and Lola. After he proved his skills by breaking into their cars undetected. I agreed to meet with him. As soon as he saw me, his chest sank. He went from slick investigator to father figure. He refused to take my money and offered me some wise words. After our talk, I was a little calmer, but that talk would provide little comfort for taming the rage I felt when engaged in heated arguments with my child's father and his woman.

The stress and abandonment had taken their toll. I wanted to hurt them both. So much so that I dreamt about it. I did more than dream about it. I made plans to fuck up the very people who had fucked me up. It was my last thought before going to sleep and the first thought when I woke up. The last straw was when the three of us got into another heated argument over my rights with my daughter and Lola's involvement. After that, all I could see was red. I put on a happy face and plotted to eliminate them both. I found solace in my plans. I started to plot their murders ... yeah, murders.

I knew how I would do it. It would be easy to get Owen alone, preferably in a car headed to East St. Louis for another night out. I would pull off on an abandoned side street or deserted lot, lure him outside the car, and pow! I already had her prints (from the investigator), and her DNA was all over his car. It would be the perfect way to get rid of them and move on. As the days passed, I became obsessed with my project. I never shared my inner thoughts or plans with anyone.

The week I planned on finishing the task approach. Little did I know that by the week's end, one person would be dead and another in critical condition, and a host of family and friends would be left with a million questions. As it turned out, I was not the only jealous person in our circle filled with rage. There was another toxic relationship brewing for disaster. Someone close to the crew and closer to Owen had carried out publicly what I had planned privately. Sitting in my bed with Tai nearby, tears poured from our eyes as we heard the horrific account of our friend's attempted murder of his girlfriend and his suicide. I cried for him, her, and myself. I went into the bathroom and repented for my darkest thoughts. I thanked God for my life, and everyone and everything in it. I thanked him for second, third, and fourth chances. I had been angry, heartbroken, embarrassed, and bruised, but nothing that I had experienced was worth such a permanent decision. What our friend had inflected on this world with his sudden absence was unthinkable. I saw the devastation on the deceased's family's and friends' faces. The kids he left behind. The hurt, sadness, and eternal loss resulting from a temporary emotion. I was depressed, but I also had too much sense and foundation to let a relationship bring this much sorrow to anyone I loved.

A few days after our friend's funeral, I was at home watching the travel channel, and an *Explore Hawaii* episode was on. The water, the picturesque sky, and the sounds of Hawaii spoke to me. In that one-hour episode, I found the strength to start over. Life is so beautiful, and I planned on experiencing the beautiful parts of it more often. People were traveling, relaxing, and enjoying their lives. Here I sat, blessed but too consumed by this relationship to appreciate it. As the host splashed through the clear blue waters of Waikiki and ate fine cuisine at a five-star resort, I, too, could someday do the same. I did not have to remain in my situation. I could go somewhere that allowed me to breathe and feel anew. A feeling I had not felt for quite a while. It was time for a change. The next day, at the office, I ordered the *AJC* and the *Houston Chronicle* and started getting my affairs in order. I'm from the "show me state," so I was going to *show* everyone that I could win with two kids. To answer Owen's question, "Where are you going with two kids?" Atlanta baby!

"A person who has been punished is not less inclined to behave in a given way; at least, he learns how to avoid punishment."

BF Skinner

FAST AND EASY

Before I left St. Louis, I applied for several positions, terminated my lease, and put in my two-week notice. I arranged for Jaimee to remain in St. Louis with my parents until I came home for Thanksgiving two months later. It was the first weekend in September of 1996. I rented a vehicle, put mine on a flatbed, and filled a 20-foot U-Haul with all my worldly possessions. My dad and Cousin Rico drove the U-Haul, and I followed. This was a big step for a 23-year-old woman with two kids in a city I had only visited a few times before. When I first arrived in Atlanta, my plan was simple—to finish college, become gainfully employed, create a side hustle that would eventually become my life's work, raise two productive and happy children, and party like a rock star. I had no order of events. It only took a second for that plan to unravel.

I was accepted to the two universities I applied to. One was a liberal arts college with nothing I wanted to major in, but I applied to it as a backup plan. And at the time, the other school only accepted one type of student loan that would leave me with a balance before I could complete registration. The way business was done in Atlanta was very different than how it was done in St. Louis. Things seemed more challenging, with more paperwork and credit checks for everything. Opening a checking account was like applying for a home loan. It felt like the city planners got together and asked, "How can we frustrate the absolute shit out of people?" Public transportation went place no one needed to go, and counties operated more like states. Atlanta was a hustle, but people moved there because there was an emphasis on education, black pride, and success. A shining city that was still gleaming and growing from the Olympics. But upon further observation, there were a lot of smoke and mirrors. Higher rent, lower wages, and extensive travel and traffic. It was the land of opportunity if you moved from New York, Connecticut, and California, but for a girl from the Midwest, the shit was out of control. Regardless of the red tape and shenanigans, I, like so many others, opted to stay. Maybe it was to prove that we could survive in this new metropolis, or maybe it was the pull of the amount of sin we could get away with anonymously.

Before I completed my move, my mom researched and located her cousin Marjorie as a point of contact once I arrived in Atlanta. I called Marjorie a week after I arrived and arranged lunch with her and her daughter Darby. We hit it off instantly. Marjorie was full of energy and cursed like a sailor; she could walk into any kitchen and, a couple of hours later, have a five-star meal prepared. Best of all, she enjoyed her life. The apple did not fall far from the tree with her daughter Darby. These two beautiful women gave me plenty of laughs, wholesome conversations, and a sense of belonging. Darby was hilarious, well-educated, had great credit, and loved her weed. She was an old soul in a young woman's body. And when she was not high or doing something newsworthy, she could be a voice of reason. I think we meshed because we both looked like law-abiding citizens, and for the most part, we were, but we were just as comfortable breaking it. We both worked for prestigious companies and dressed the part. However, we spent about 35% of our time clubbing, drinking, and dating, 30% getting into trouble, and the remaining 35% on family, faith, and work. I have no regrets, but the repercussions of some of the shit we did still lingers. Those years provided distress, frustration, lost opportunities, and bad luck. It also provided its share of side-splitting laughter and pure entertainment.

Case and point, during my first and only Freaknik experience, Dee, another friend, and I were stuck in a mob of traffic. As participants, we were caught amidst booty shaking, gyrating, and every lude gesture you could imagine. I did not understand the point of having some strange guys see you naked (for free) and take advantage of you in the middle of the street or in the back of a pickup truck for all to see. Freaknik was pure unadulterated live porn. Sodom and Gomorrah. It was entertaining but a bit much for my liking.

One night during the festivities, I grew tired and agitated sitting in traffic for hours with ass in my face. So, I attempted to make my way through traffic to get out. I spotted a perfect opening, and as I started moving over, this car came out of nowhere and almost hit me. The vehicle's occupants were females; the smell of weed drifted from their open windows as they danced, laughed, and were unaware of our near collision. However, I was fully aware and annoyed, so I honked to get their attention. They started talking shit and gesturing at us, so naturally, we returned the favor. One of the girls was overly animated but seemed to quiet down as I parked my car and opened my door.

At that time, the driver of that vehicle made an aggressive maneuver that placed them just out of our reach. Not satisfied with how the spat ended, we were determined to catch up with them. When we finally did, Darby asked me to get as close as possible so she could pepper spray inside their car. Sounded like a good plan. I worked my way closer, and we began the stare-down and shit-talking to get their attention again. Darby was in the passenger seat, and Sherry was in the back. I guess it was the alcohol, but neither of us noticed that Darby's window was up.

When that fool opened fire with her can of pepper spray, it hit our window and blew back through our car like a firebomb. Suddenly, Sherry was in the back gasping for air and spitting up, my face was on fire, and I couldn't see shit. I had to slam the car into park and jump out just to breathe. Darby looked like she was crying and covering her nose with her shirt. She was feverishly trying to escape, but we had pulled so close to the other vehicle her door would not open. The joke was on us, I couldn't see them, but I damn sure heard the laughter and high-fives of the occupants in the targeted vehicle. We must have look like a bunch of idiots. Here we were—the three amigos—victims of our own ambush while the other car sped off laughing uncontrollably. My cousin had sprayed her own damn team. What a night! These girls were crazy and dangerous, and I was hooked.

My first job in Atlanta was at the local newspaper. I worked in the advertising department, where we placed ads over the phone for individuals and businesses. When someone opened an account to place an ad, we collected an excessive amount of information, including social security number, credit card number, address, date of birth, and more. While working here, I was befriended by Sabrina from Boston. We became close acquaintances and went out from time to time. What I liked most about Sabrina, besides her cool accent, was that she was always impeccably dressed from head to toe. During lunch one afternoon, Sabrina told me she had access to clothes, shoes, bags, perfume, and more. At the time, Atlanta was a breeding ground for behind-the-scenes crime, identity theft, credit card fraud, mortgage fraud, and the like. Crimes I like to call "bitch ass ness" crimes, where you screw someone without them having an opportunity to defend themselves. Sabrina showed me how she would capture callers' information and later use it to open accounts. It seemed easy enough as I thought; h*ell, I could always use more stuff.* I was amazed at how easy it was to obtain things using other people's information or money. I am sure this is not the same theory Warren Buffet and Bill Gates were referring to regarding "other's people money," but you get how addictive this seemingly faceless crime could become.

Not easily satisfied, I was determined to figure out how to take this inch of the hustle and get mile-long results. The clothes were great, but more money and other retail necessities would be better. To use this information just for outfits seemed like a waste. So, I devised a plan to get more bang for our buck. On my first Christmas in Atlanta, I purchased almost $20k worth of stuff (i.e., shoes, clothes, perfume, outings, furniture, jewelry, home décor, and everything in between). At 24 years of age, I thought the world was my oyster and things would only get better. As a 24-year-old black woman, I had visited almost every store within a 10-mile radius of my home and convinced people that I had the established credit and means of the 48-year-old woman I was portraying. My tools were a pair of cheap glasses, a wig, and a boatload of confidence. The timing was perfect; it was the Christmas season, and stores handed out instant credit like candy. My plans would have failed if just one employee had done little due diligence (like asking for a license). Instead, I was met by eager sales associates with quotas to hit and bonuses to earn.

After the Christmas heist, I became the go-to person for new hustles. I would plan and execute them with precision. I had a clean record, dressed nicely, spoke proper English, and was attractive. Piece of cake.

On top of that, I was a good employee. Also, I had become an addict and wanted all I could get. The adrenaline from getting away with our actions provided a false sense of power. For a while, it was a better high than alcohol. Then, Sabrina got a part-time job at a popular women's retailer. She wanted me to come to her store one weekend that she thought she would be working by herself. She said I could bring a couple of people to get everything we desired in that one visit. I told my cousin and Sherry the plans, and everything was set.

On the day of our "shopping opportunity," I reached out to Sabrina, as instructed, to confirm a good time; it was later discovered that after I placed my call to her, Darby had called four additional times to confirm the same. The number of calls for Sabrina piqued the store manager's interest. So much so that she intercepted one of the calls placed by Darby. She pretended to be Sabrina and listened as Darby dumb ass reviewed our plans to rob this store to the store manager. Before we could leave the house,

Sabrina called b to inform me of her termination. She had been fired because of my cousin's in-depth phone conversation with her boss. I was livid I asked Darby why she thought it was a good idea to call someone at work excessively?

To which she had no reply. I needed to know why going over a criminal plan over the phone was a good idea. We were lucky no one went to jail that time. The store manager could have allowed things to play out and contacted the authorities to meet us at the front door upon leaving her store. My relationship with Sabrina was forever strained from that point, and I had to reconsider who I did dirt with going forward. But instead of replacing my cousin or stopping altogether, I tightened things up and gave what I believed were better directions. But no longer with Darby. Once was enough. A normal person would have conceded, but not me; I went and applied to the same store (different location) and masterminded the hustle from the inside. I was great at it too. The amount of merchandise we stole was enough to open our boutique. I had tags for weeks. My ability to manipulate situations gave me a feeling like nothing had before.

I graduated from retail to money orders when presented with yet another opportunity by the other third of our threesome. Sherry was an acquaintance of a guy who owned a convenience store. It was his idea originally. He would sell a block of money orders and later file a claim against them. He would claim they had been stolen or unaccounted for. He gave us a timeframe in which to use them before he made a report. Reporting the money order stolen or unaccounted for was for his protection but was a risk for the person cashing the check. It took a while for the issuer or the merchants that were now victims to get wind of it, but once they were reported, anyone associated with these money orders had just committed a felony (based on the amount). We had stacks of them too. At one point, we got a map and planned to hit Tennessee, Alabama, Florida, and every part of Georgia. The idea was to hit one check-cashing store at a time. That way, we looked like victims when the money orders were stolen because it was just a one-time transaction. However, we never considered that any investigator with half a brain would first have all the affected merchants send in a copy of the IDs of the people cashing the money orders...duh. If that happened, they would see our smiling faces, soon to be wanted in multiple states for felony fraud and theft by deception. Good luck with that. The first stop was my nearby check cashers. I walked in with checks and walked out with $2000 in under 8 minutes.

Later that evening, after I put Jaimee to bed. I was enjoying a cocktail and watching TV, when Sherry came by ready to cash her second series of money orders. I thoroughly explained to her how to carry out the plan flawlessly, she could go to any check-cashing center she wanted to, *except one* (the one I went to earlier that day). I reiterated that we could not visit the same store twice because the numbers on the money orders were consecutive, and all the amounts matched, which would raise a red flag. She waved my instructions off and swore she had another store in mind. She then grabbed *my* car keys and was out the door because her car had no gas. I was like, "Bitch, aren't you about to go get paid? Fill up then," but she was already starting my car and putting it in reverse. I watched her turn the corner and return to my movie and cocktail. After about forty minutes passed with no call or sign of Sherry, I began to worry. If I had my car, I would have gone to look for her. I made another cocktail and began pacing the living room. As "What's love got to do with it" climaxed, something told me to look outside. I peeked through my patio blinds and saw people in dark clothes and car/vans with no lights on. I squinted to get a clearer view through the small slit in the blinds; the images became clearer, as the lights on top of the police cars signaled to me, that this would be a long night for somebody. Before I could finish that thought, there was a loud knock at my front door, then another one followed by "Cobb County Police."

I had never been so freaking scared in my life. My heartbeat like a drum, and my chest was on fire. This was adrenaline, but a different one than what I felt earlier cashing those money orders.

Jaimee was asleep in her room, no one else was there, and I had a shit load of money orders in the living room. I felt the heat of fear run through my body as the temperature inside me rose. Instinctively I hid the money orders under the couch and opened the door. Not one, not two, but three sheriffs/officers were trying to confirm my identity, which I confirmed. At that point, I hoped that if I cooperated (to a certain point), I would be spared for good behavior. Like a dumb ass, I allowed them into my home. I could see by the look on their faces they were impressed with my living quarters, both cleanliness and furnishings. One of the officers broke the awkward silence, saying he had my associate in the back of his car. They had picked her up from a local check-cashing store where she had attempted to cash some stolen money orders. He went further to say she had already confessed and pointed to me as the ringleader. I chuckled and said, well, I guess you can add a false statement to her record because that could not be further from the truth. As a matter of fact, why are you here again?" They went on to explain how the store clerk showed them my ID from earlier and the four money orders I had cashed. I was like, "Okay, so what does that mean?" I tried to act confused, but they shared the unlikely coincidence that acquaintances (Sherry and I) both had been taken by different people and just happened to have money orders from the same batch, in numerical order, cashing them on the same day at the same store. All I could do to keep from agreeing was to keep quiet while thinking of scenarios where Sherry could disappear without it being traced back to me.

They looked through my house (very carefully), in the kitchen and bathroom drawers; the loud voices and commotion woke Jaimee up, and her little cuteness came out half smiling. I could see the disappointment in the police officers' eyes as they collectively took deep breaths upon seeing my baby girl. To top it off, she had the nerve to say, "Not again," as if I was some mob boss who stayed in trouble with the law. I'm unsure if they heard her, but I almost passed out. They politely asked me if I had someone who could get her (that was nice, they could have taken her to DFAC or something). I told them I had relatives who lived in the same complex. They allowed me to drop Jaimee off at Marjorie's and Darby's. To be honest, up until that point, I thought I would get off with a warning or court date. Nope, handcuffed and a police ride to Cobb County Adult Detention Center, the first of many visits to this facility.

Our big money scheme was over before it got started. After only $8500 fucking dollars, I received my first experience with Georgia law. Within the confines of Cobb County detention center, Sherry and I sat side by side for the remainder of the night in the holding cell, mainly because we were trying to stay warm. I don't think either of us knew how severe this was, especially me. We sat and cracked jokes about the first thing we would do when we got out, what food we would eat, take a long bath, and have a drink. Hell! We acted as if we had already been in prison for a couple of years. Sherry made her calls from the phone outside the holding cell. I made sure she included me in her plans for freedom. Since I was not from Georgia, it would be more difficult for my family in Missouri to spring me out. So, I had to rely on the kindness of my newfound friend and her family to put their name on the line to set me free. Otherwise, I would have been done. Thank God I didn't have to cross that bridge. Not that time, anyway. I was never mad at myself for breaking the law. I was more upset that we got caught than anything else.

After Sherry's big talk about being so fucking street smart and a talented manipulator, her ignorant ass walked into the store where she was forbidden to go in. I felt like Ray Liotta's character in *Goodfellas*. For those who don't know the movie, Ray Liotta's character is dealing drugs outside his mob circle; in one scene, he calls one of his drug mules, who had flown in and was at his house waiting on him. In his conversation with her, he repeated no fewer than 50 times that she should not make any calls from the house phone. He even went as far as to have her repeat him. Simple, right? Now, what did she do? As soon as she hung up, she picked up the same damn house phone and made the connection call from his house. Hours later, the feds flooded the property and took everyone into custody. Ray's drug mule and Sherry were cut from the same fucking thread; what a pair of buffoons.

We got out later that next afternoon. It did not matter to me, though. I was not going to stop. I was going to get better. Months later, our attorneys got us into the first offender's program, where our conviction would be erased provided, we maintained clean records and violated no laws for the next five years. Okay.

Regardless of the mounting troubles we created together, I still had a blast with Darby and Sherry. We were bad for each other, but we provided entertainment and great stories for those who knew us. Another example, my employer gave me two free passes to a Marital Arts academy, so naturally, I invited Darby. On the day of our first visit to the academy, this crazy woman picked me up wearing a braided wig. I do not have anything against wigs, but this is before the functional ones used today. Why would you wear a wig to karate class? I immediately let her know my concern and disapproval. But in true Darby fashion, she replied, "Nah' cuzz, it's on tight, and I got bobby pins to secure it; we good."

I looked at her with utter bemusement. "Okay, let's hope so," was my response. I asked her to double-check to ensure her hair was good for the duration; she flicked me off, laughed, and gently tugged at the side of the wig for reassurance. Upon entering the lobby, I gave my name and tickets; the lady at the front desk asked if we had ever taken classes before and showed us to our room. Every room had three full walls of windows, for onlookers' enjoyment. We were instructed to remove our shoes, and the instructor gave a respectful bow to acknowledge us (so I did the same in return); Darby, on the other hand, reached out to the bowing man and attempted to give him dap (which is a hand bump of sorts used in place of the traditional handshake). Inappropriate in this setting. You should have seen the confused look on the instructor's face.

The place was packed with students and spectators, and as the only black people besides the instructor, we stood out like sore thumbs. I could only imagine what the instructor was thinking of two black girls coming in late, smelling like weed, dressed more for the mall than to work out. The class was performing the warm-up, so we joined in. I made it my intention to separate myself from Darby. During the warm-up stretches, she kept moaning and pointing out how flexible everyone else was. Once done stretching, the instructor wanted us to pair up so we could spar. I quickly paired up with a guy next to me to avoid being paired with her. Darby searched the room for an available partner. The instructions were to have one person hold a padded bag against their chest while the other kicked it. This was to build up the core of the person holding the bag through resistance training while providing strength training and cardio for the person kicking. My partner and I were sparring and getting better with each count. We performed a series of kicks alternating between us. After a round of kicks we had to switch partners. Before I could even move, Darby stood before me, ready to go. Since our time to switch was brief, I resisted the urge to point her in another direction.

Following directions IS NOT a side effect of being in an induced state of mind. Darby was the first to kick while I held the protective cushion, no problem. But when we switched, things took a turn for the worse. "Hut three hut four ... kick! Hut three, hut four ... kick!" The first series almost sent Darby flying on her ass. I was like, "What the hell are you doing? Defend yourself, girl!"

Her reply was, "Damn, cuzz, you mad or something? You're kicking like Bruce Lee!"

"Darb, hold the mat and keep your balance. Use your core and push back!" She gave a sly grin and nodded to signal that she was ready for action.

The instructors shouted the count, "Hut three, hut four, hut," then dead silence. After the last kick, Darby lost her balance, and her head snapped back (she was being dramatic); all I recall was her wig hitting the ground and Darby looking at me like it was my hair on the floor. An embarrassing hush fell over the class as her wig, and matted hair became the focus of everyone's attention. To add insult to injury, Darby picked the wig up like no one noticed and put it back on. Unfortunately, her wig was on backward, and the braids stuck up like the predators. I was frozen and still in my stance when she dared to ask me to fix it for her. I exhaled and reached out to turn the wig around and tighten it. I also made it a point not to look at anyone else at that moment. I was torn between peeing on myself from holding in a deep belly laugh and absolute shame. After getting Darby's wig straightened, I motioned the instructor to proceed. A few people had turned away, and from the shaking of their shoulders, I could tell they were engaged in the best laugh of their week. I'm sure those people shared that story multiple times to anyone who would listen, in the days that followed. I wished Scotty could have beamed me up, or I could have clicked my heels and ended up in Kansas, but no such luck would be extended to me on that day.

My pride would not allow me to leave class early. But when class was over, I made a mad dash to the exit like the place was on fire. I thought Darby was behind me, but she stayed behind to go over the upcoming schedule with the instructor and director. Wow! what a hilarious woman.

A lot went on during the first six months of my Peach State residency. Another one of our escapades took place on Saturday evening. Sherry and I planned a night out, so I took Jaimee to a late-night daycare center around the corner from my place, where she attended from time to time. We ended up at a club off Memorial Drive, closer to Sherry's house and far from mine. We tossed back drinks, danced, and mingled. Sherry left with some dude she met, and I stayed to enjoy the rest of my night. About an hour later, I wrapped my night up and exit the club. As I dug in my purse for my keys, I realized they were gone, and so was my vehicle. I immediately panic. I thought *this crazy bitch left in my car, leaving me stranded*. I dialed her number vigorously as I tried to compose myself. I kept getting her voicemail. I was unsure of what to do because I lived more than 30 minutes away, and the late-night daycare was due to close within the hour. Finally, a guy who worked at the club saw me freaking out and offered to take me to retrieve my vehicle. With limited options, I accepted. I got into his car and provided the directions to Sherry's place.

As I was talking, I noticed we were going in the opposite direction, seemingly with no plans to make a U-turn. I asked him if he was taking a shortcut, but he did not respond. Any remnants of alcohol left my body as I realized I had made a horrible mistake by getting into this stranger's car. I had to think quickly and keep things from going from bad to worse. While reaching into my purse, I said with all the conviction I could muster, "If you do not turn this fucking car around right now, I will fuck you up! I told you I must get my car and my daughter."

Without making a fuss, he said calmly, "Alright, calm down; I was just going to make a quick stop." I kept my hand on my imaginary gun inside my purse until I got out of the car.

I jumped out without the car coming to a complete stop once we got back to the club. I whispered, "Thank you, Jesus," under my breath and took my phone out to call Sherry. Before it rang, she pulled onto the lot, blowing the horn to get my attention. I didn't have time for explanations, apologies, or kicking her ass; I had to get to my daughter. So, without offering to take her home, I snatched my keys, jumped in my car, and peeled out. It was like I couldn't drive fast enough. The roads were slick from the downpour earlier that day, but I couldn't worry about all that, as I hit speeds over 80 miles per hour.

Minutes later, I was merging onto interstate 75 north from interstate 20 when it happened. Once again, the world was moving in slow motion, and I was a spectator. I had lost control of my vehicle. I locked eyes with a passenger of another car in the far-left lane as mine began to spin out of control. The headlights of the oncoming traffic were the last thing I remembered before slamming into a wall and blacking out.

I heard voices and tried to make out what they were saying. My eyes were closed, but I was not asleep. I heard a man's voice say, "This is a drunk driver that came in this morning." I slowly pulled my wrist towards my chest to see if handcuffs constrained them. "Thank you, Jesus," I whispered under my breath for the second time that night, "no handcuffs." Upon realizing where I was, I started to panic again. "What time is it? Where is my daughter? Oh, God! She's only five!" A nurse ran over to calm me down, but it was too late. I had no idea how long I was passed out, but I knew I had never made it to the daycare. I explained my situation to the staff, and a nurse looked up the number and spoke to the woman waiting at the daycare with Jaimee. She explained what had taken place and confirmed that Jaimee was okay. I called Darby to arrange for her to pick Jaimee up. With that taken care of, I passed back out.

Later that day, I was brought up to speed by the doctor attending to my injuries. I had suffered a busted forehead (courtesy of the windshield), and I was struck in the chest by the airbags and was thrown from the driver's side to the passenger's side from the impact (no seatbelt). He further put me at ease that no other vehicles were involved. Darby and Jaimee walked in as he was wrapping up. Darby had to bring me a change of clothes, since I was unconscious when I got to the ER, my clothes had been cut off for safety reasons; After being discharged, my first stop was the impound. When the attendant walked us over to my once beautiful car, we all gasped. The engine was in the front seat, the entire driver-side door had been pushed in, and both airbags had deployed. God does watch over babies and fools; Damn, I was lucky. No seatbelt, excessive speeds, impaired, and standing water—a deadly combination. Jaimee started to cry when she saw the entire car; I guess even at five years of age, she was smart enough to know her mom was one fortunate lady. If only she knew just how many times I had and would be spared. We picked something up for dinner, filled my prescription, and went home.

A week before the accident, I started a new job at a global computer company. The first two weeks of training were mandatory, and we had just completed the first. I had a busted forehead and major pain, but I had to go; I could not miss training. I got sad looks and questions from my co-workers, but I had little to say. A week later, I received a call through the company's 800 number. I was called over to my manager's desk to take it. The voice on the other end sounded relieved. He said, "I have tried everything to contact you." He offered his name and asked me if I remembered anything about the night of my accident. I raised an eyebrow and said, "Not really." He introduced himself as a CNN employee; he said he witnessed the entire thing. He told me how my car slid from one side of the highway to the other, hitting the wall each time and finally coming to a rest facing oncoming traffic with me slumped over in the passenger seat. He told me how scared he was when he got out of his car and ran towards me on the interstate. He said my car was smoking, and he was unsure if it was mechanical or the airbags. He hesitated as he tried to figure out the best way to help just in case of a hidden fire; as he got closer, he realized that the smoke was coming from the airbags. He climbed in the back seat, waiting with me for over forty-five minutes before the ambulance finally arrived. He went further to say that his goal was to keep me conscious until help arrived because of the injury to my head. We talked about my daughter, my new job (that is how he found me), and how upset my parents would be once they found out about this. Before we hung up, he gave me his name, title, and phone number and asked me to keep in touch. I did not know what to say except, "Thank you for everything." As far as keeping in touch, I never did.

The shenanigans with Darby and Sherry were getting old. And for one reason or another, we got into a dispute that never was resolved and parted ways. I cannot remember why we fell out, but we did. I recall wanting to get revenge or kick their asses on sight. There was always some bullshit with these two. For the best part of seven years, we never crossed paths. Grocery stores, concerts, restaurants, clubs, gas stations, nail salons, malls … nothing. The beef between Darby and I had gotten so petty that I called her job and told them that she was wearing an ankle monitor (which was true). I also thought I saw her in the parking lot of my job when I was leaving for lunch with a co-worker. Later that afternoon, when I got into my vehicle, I had a cigarette butt burn in my driver's seat where I had left the window cracked. I blamed her because she was the one person in my circle that smoked.

I did run into Marjorie, Darby's mom, at church about five years later. I was pleasantly surprised and a little embarrassed that it had been so long since we spoke. After a brief chat, we vowed to stay in touch, and she disappeared into the sanctuary. It would be the last time I saw her. Sometime after that exchange, Marjorie was diagnosed with a rare cancer. I felt my heart sink for Darby and the dispute that made me miss out on the fun we always had together. It was my uncle who delivered the news of her diagnosis. It would be my mom who delivered the news of her passing. Marjorie had fought a long, hard battle with cancer, but in the end, she decided to end the battle. The death of Marjorie brought Darby and me back into each other lives. I could not fathom the pain and emptiness she must have felt. She and her mom were two peas in a pod. Marjorie was the coolest person anyone could meet, and I was always proud when I spoke of her. She was a world-class cook, a realist, and a diva. There will never be another like her.

Unable to attend the funeral in St. Louis, I wanted Darby to know I was thinking of her. My mom suggested I write a letter to express my condolences since all the letters and cards would be shared with the family. So that is what I did. On the night of Marjorie's funeral, my phone rang, on the other end was a familiar voice… It was Darby. We talked for about forty minutes and made plans to meet up. After almost seven years of no contact, Darby and I were about to be back in stride again. Timing is everything. We were both more mature, plus neither one could remember what initiated our fallout, nor did we care. Secretly, the passing of Marjorie still hurts. She was a vital part of my early survival in

Atlanta, and I don't think I ever thanked her for that. I hope she knows now. Thank you, Marjorie. Rest well, cousin, I love you.

BORN THIS WAY?

My first taste of "crime" did not start in Atlanta. It started one holiday season when I was about five years of age. Madear had a particularly beautiful and original Christmas ornament. Since I spent so much time there, I had plenty of time to dream of having it in my possession. Instead of just asking if I could put it on our tree at home or if I could have it, I devised a plan to relieve my grandmother of her beautiful ornament. One evening, when no one was looking, I quietly removed the ornament from her tree and tucked it safely in my oversized winter coat. The next day, my granny asked my mom about the missing ornament. I stayed silent and even acted dumbfounded when questioned about it. A couple of days later, my mom called me into the dining room, holding the prettiest ornament I had ever seen. "Where did you get this from? Didn't I ask you if you had seen Madear's ornament?" I lied and said I asked for it, which worsened things. I got my butt whooped for that incident and still had to return the prettiest ornament I had ever seen back to Madear with my head hung low in shame. The moral of that story is all that glitters is not gold. What I thought would bring me joy only brought shame and guilt.

To make matters worse, as beautiful as the ornament was, I could not enjoy its beauty because I had to keep it hidden. Teachable moment here. My mom and grandma never said the words thief and liar to my face, but it was the unspoken truth. Too bad I didn't learn at five what I have come to know decades later.

There would be an endless supply of "the prettiest ornament I have ever seen" throughout my life. I resisted most of the time, but old habits die hard, and so do pathologies. I continued that deceitful behavior for a long time. I didn't always demonstrate it, but it was there, lying dormant. Atlanta provided many opportunities to get things fast, but just like that ornament, easy come, easy go. But, as I said earlier, I was hooked. After all, many had come before me and turned their wrongdoings into profitable businesses. I wanted the clothes, cars, and cash, and I wanted them in a millisecond of what working a nine-to-five would bring. So, I put myself in a position to influence the hustle. Atlanta was brazened with crime. People were buying—homes and cars and getting high-limit credit cards without all the red tape. Atlanta was a breeding ground for white-collar crime.

I worked hard to perfect my craft; I got jobs where I could get money and merchandise simultaneously. I took so much from one of my second jobs that I filled up two large storages with the merchandise. I had everything from diamond earrings, watches, pool tables, ping-pong tables, stainless steel grills, and more. My escapades eventually caught up with me and landed me in hot water with the law for a second time. In this case, I was overconfident and used my manager's employee login on a return slip valued at $864. I used that same slip to purchase a diamond ring I had been eyeballing. It was pure greed. I had more than enough merchandise and a couple of canisters full of large bills.

My downfall was my cockiness. It took one thoughtless purchase to bring the whole system down on my head. I walked into another store branch and made the purchase. Typically, this would not have raised any flags, but I used a substantial-sized voucher to complete the transaction. Note: it pays to listen to the small voice that tells you not to do something. Once I pulled out the voucher, I felt that the bitch ringing up the sale was a noisy goody two shoes. I was right; unbeknownst to me, I was put under surveillance at work because of that purchase. The salesperson reported the transaction to my home store, and about a week later, as the store was closing, I was called into the back room. They pressed me about the ring and additional merchandise. They said they had me on camera buying the ring and could produce a video to seal my fate. While all this was taking place, I thought to myself, *if your dumb assess sat back and let me steal all that shit, then everybody in this room needs to be arrested or fired.* My manager said all they wanted was the merchandise, and if I returned it within 48 hours, they would not press charges. I thought, *wouldn't that be an admission of guilt? So, I'm supposed to return some stolen shit I have not admitted to stealing and trust you will let me walk? Okay ... wait for it.* They let me go home that night, assuring me that I had 48 hours to return any and everything, or they would press charges.

I was in a bit of a jam, especially since I was already on probation through the first offender's program from the money order scheme. The thing about first offenders is that it allows those who have never been in trouble the opportunity to keep their conviction off their record provided they pay all their fines/fees and do not get any new charges during the probationary period, usually 12 months, (not even a speeding ticket). Once you complete the assigned time, your record will be deleted of the offense. The arrest will never go away, but the outcome will not be listed. The more I thought about the repercussions, the more nervous I got. I never went back to that job again. After the 48 hours expired, I was on the run. Once they filed a warrant for my arrest, my first offenders' safety net would be revoked, and if the police picked me up, I would sit in jail indefinitely. I spent the next eight months looking over my shoulder. However, I still managed to purchase a home, leave the company I worked for, and still party like a rock star. It is not like I was on America's Most Wanted, but if I got caught, I was going on an all-expenses-paid vacation to jail.

DOING THE MOST

"Who is this? What happened? I did what!" This was my response to the guy on the other end of the phone. His name was Chuck, and I had partied with him and his boys the night before. Club 112 Saturday night VIP. Drinking, smoking, and having a great time. My friend, Danielle, aka Stacey Dash, because she had a strong resemblance, and I were hanging out and caught the eye of an NBA player. We hung with him and his entourage in his VIP section, then rode in his limo to get something to eat, followed by the after-party at their hotel. I don't remember much after that, except I puked, was escorted to the limo, and was taken to my car. The above phone call came around 3:00 p.m. the next afternoon. The guy said, "Wow, I didn't know the ladies get down like that in St. Louis." I was mortified. He commented that he loved my pink thongs and that all the guys looked forward to seeing me again I was on the phone with a guy I vaguely remembered, recounting what I believed to be my sexual exploits. I was sick to my stomach and felt violated and slutty. I was ashamed to show my face in public. I might as well have been wearing a scarlet letter as far as I was concerned.

The conversation stayed in my head all week. I avoided entertaining my co-workers at work with my weekend escapades like I usually did. Finally, I decided it was time to make a change. I had not heard from Danielle since that night, and I assumed she was upset with me. I was too embarrassed to reach out to her for fear that she would confirm what Chuck had said earlier that week over the phone. Disgraced, so much so, I recommitted my life to Christ that following Sunday. I felt like the prodigal child coming home as I walked down the aisle to repent of my sins. The crazy thing about blackouts, you never really get the whole story in a timely fashion, if at all. I was so nervous that one of my fun boys may have been in the congregation. At this point, not even salvation provided any comfort for having slept with multiple strangers the week before. Damn, the drinking and then blacking out had me playing Russian roulette with my life again.

It would be more than a week before Danielle came to my job to have lunch with Katie and me. Once seated at our table, they started smiling and then laughing. I thought, *"what the heck is so damn funny?"* they finally let me in on the cruel joke Danielle and the guys had played on me about sleeping with them. They intended to scare the shit out of me so I would never get that drunk again. "I may not be there to take care of you next time," she said. Point taken. It was like I had been cleansed of all my sins with one carefully planned conversation. I thought to myself, *thank you, Jesus,* followed by, *Maybe I'll go out to celebrate tonight.*

The place was called Otto's. It was an extremely popular hangout for professional athletes and beautiful women. On Sunday night, it was the place to see and be seen. Buckhead nightlife was *the* life. I went alone because I knew that being a single lady in the club had advantages. No waiting in line, free drinks, easy access to VIPs, and no girlfriend drama. On Sunday nights, there was nothing but space and opportunity. He was from Baltimore and stood six feet six inches tall. He was not a professional athlete but threw his money around just the same. We met on my usual Sunday night trip to Otto's, and two weeks later, I was on a flight to Baltimore to spend a weekend with him. Kenny was a true gentleman. Before allowing him to book the flight, we agreed on sleeping arrangements. We hadn't been intimate prior to the trip, and I made it clear we wouldn't start just because I was there. We dined, shopped, and took in the sights from Baltimore to DC. I was maturing and cared how people saw me. I could travel and enjoy myself without over-indulging because that had always been the easier thing to do. I was experiencing intimacy instead of sex, and that made me desirable. Of course, Kenny wanted to have sex; hell, I would have thought differently of him had he not. But he respected my boundaries, and we had a blast. Before leaving, we made plans for him to visit me in Atlanta a few months later during Super Bowl week.

January rolled around quickly, and it was time for Super Bowl in the ATL. Kenny made it before the ice storm did. At the time, my acquaintance Danielle, the chick from the 112 fiasco, was "crashing" in my lower level. This was perfect timing, with all the people in town, there were no rental cars available and mine was in the shop until the following Monday. So, Danielle's vehicle came in handy. The week leading up to Super Bowl was awesome; the parties were epic, and the city was festive. Unfortunately, Super Bowl weekend was a disaster. The ice storm was worse than predicted. The East Coast was covered in ice. I mean, everything was frozen over. Tai and her guy had planned on driving down but had to cancel because of the dangerous road conditions.

Everything from that point on was at our own risk. And risks we took. Super Bowl weekend translates into whatever the hell you want it to translate into. People tend to lose their inhibitions during the Superbowl festivities. Married, gay, straight, black, white, women, men, beautiful, ugly ... did not matter. Despite the warnings to stay off the roads, we still enjoyed ourselves. Although dangerous, the city covered in ice was something to behold; it was like a flawless jewel glistening in the night. On Super Bowl eve, Kenny, Danielle, and I ventured into the city. I lived in a suburb of Atlanta, and my regular 30 minutes commute became a two-hour trip. But the draw of sexy affluent men, beautiful scantily clad women, and enough alcohol to submerge the city was more powerful than the thought of...dying. We were not the only ones risking bodily injury to have a good time, the parking lots were packed, and the lines were long. We clubbed hopped around the area, danced, laughed, drank, and were merrier than we should have been in the hazardous conditions.

We decided to head back home around 3:00 a.m. At the time, our location was at a popular club near the Buckhead/Midtown area. We hopped on interstate 85S to head home (Danielle behind the wheel). This route would get us home quicker with less traffic and fewer hills. As we got on the ramp to 85, the darkness hid the icy road beneath us. Alcohol also played a part in our speed and recklessness. Danielle hit the road going about 45 miles per hour. As we merged onto the interstate, there was an influx of cars, all moving at a snailass pace (for a good reason). Danielle took it upon herself to rush past everyone else, and that's when it happened. The tread on our tires proved worthless against the ice and performed more like rollerblades than grippers. As we became aware of our mistake, Kenny screamed from the back seat,

"Shit! Don't press the brea—"

His words fell on a discombobulated Danielle. She fought to regain control of the now spinning vehicle. It was like something out of the *Matrix;* everything except us was moving in slow motion. We were on fast-forward. I glanced to my right then to my left as cars started to stop, and drivers stared at the inevitable. My eyes met Danielle's, then Kenny's, like we wanted to remember the faces of those we would perish with. No heartbeat, no brain waves, no breath, just a twirling car, an embankment, and a road of ice. We held on in silence, embracing for impact as the SUV swirled from the middle of the interstate towards the embankment. A short wall that misrepresented the 200-foot drop it concealed.

I heard that your life flashes before you right before you die. I thought to myself; *Maybe I will live tonight*. The only thing that flashed before me was the picture of a tilting SUV plastered on the warning sticker on the passenger side mirror. The sticker stuck out as if to say, "You were warned." Just as quickly as we had lost control of the truck, it suddenly stopped, literally two inches from the wall. Can you believe it! No damage to the truck, no one else was hit, no cops, nothing. It looked like we just pulled over on the shoulder. As the blood started to run back through our veins, I could hear a small collective sigh of relief from the other occupants of the truck. For what seemed even longer than the spinning ordeal, we sat in what I thought was silence but soon understood it to be shock. My mouth and eyes were as wide as the road that lay before us as I clinched the passenger seat's overhead handle with a Kung fu-like grip. To our immediate right was the dark and airy drop, which a minute ago, if not for the good Lord himself, was sure to be our brief graves; by all reasonable accounts, that truck should have flipped over that wall. We had survived. I started to believe I was a feline and had nine lives.

The sound of cursing, flashing lights, and car horns shook us out of our daze. Danielle slowly pulled off at about three miles per hour as we began our voyage back home. We made it off interstate 85 only to merge on 75N with about an hour of tense travel on our journey to the house. What a night. Not one word had been spoken since we were spared; the adrenaline must have worn off Danielle, and the depressant effects of the alcohol kicked in because when I looked over at the driver's seat, this bitch was asleep! Kenny and I must have noticed this simultaneously because I opened my mouth to speak and heard his voice. "What the fuck? Your ass sleep! Are you fucking kidding me right now?" He demanded she put the car in park and switch seats with him. Kenny said it with so much vigor it startled both Danielle and me. She was so startled she swerved into the left lane, narrowly missing the median, and we avoided kissing a wall for the second time that night. As instructed, she parked the truck right in the middle of the frozen interstate and climbed in the back seat.

The next day, I went to the grocery store and cooked breakfast and lunch. No need to go into the city just for food. After all, we had survived the previous night and did not need more close calls. The weather started to break with the appearance of the sun, but we were far from good road conditions. We had plans to attend a Super Bowl party that evening at a hotel. Danielle said she had to pick her guy up and would be back shortly. We thought nothing of it. We got dressed, fixed a cocktail, and waited and waited and waited. Our calls to Danielle went unanswered as we sat in my family room while the Saint Louis Rams claimed their first Super Bowl win by beating the Tennessee Titans (23-16). Although it was a great game, we were the ones that got played. Danielle never came back. The amount of profanity from Kenny's mouth and mine about Danielle's outright disrespect was enough to make a sailor blush.

Now for me, I could easily get over the disappointment, but for Kenny, who, even though he did not go to the game, flew from Baltimore to partake in the local festivities, it was more of a challenge. I felt bad for him; he had been patient and cool the entire time. But for what it is worth, I'm sure this had to be one of his most memorable Super Bowl experiences to date. Now he would return home with a good story that had nothing to do with partying, celebrities, or the game. We stayed in contact and laughed at our Super Bowl ordeal quite often, although we never saw each other again.

LEFT, RIGHT, LEFT

I'd been in my new home for just over three months. At that point, I avoided getting caught for so long that I let my guard down and behaved like a woman who did not have law enforcement looking for her. This brings me to Keith. Before I met Kenny, Keith was crucial in aiding and abetting me when I was on the run from the law. Keith put me in a hotel for over a month while I completed my home purchase. "Why was I in a hotel, you asked?" I ended up staying in a hotel after a plain-clothes cop came looking for me at my place. As promised, the warrant from my previous employer had been executed. I knew I had to face the music one day, but with each passing day, it became harder and harder to accept. I had two children, a new mortgage, and responsibilities. I didn't have time to be incarcerated. The law would have to wait.

One evening I was headed out to meet Keith and some friends; I was all dolled up, the moon roof was open, the fresh summer breeze was gently blowing, and I was sipping Hennessey and Coke from my crystal glass. Life was good, and then it wasn't. The lights came out of nowhere, and the good life was over. The male officer got out of his vehicle and proceeded to my window. I quickly sprayed the car with air freshener and place my glass inside the armrest. He asked for my license and registration and went back to his vehicle. I made several calls while waiting for him to return because I knew how it would end. As I awaited the inevitable, I took off my jewelry, took a big swig of my drink and turned on some music. Shortly after, he returned with the expected news. I don't know who was more disappointed, him or me. He was so apologetic for the inconvenience of having to do his job.

"Ma'am, are you on probation?"

To which I did not reply, and he continued,

"Unfortunately, my system tells me I must take you in for probation violation. Do you have anyone that can come get your vehicle?"

I let him know that my boyfriend could get it. I said he lived far away, so it would take him a while.

"Well, my supervisor told me to have it towed, but if he picks it up,

I'll park it, and he can come to get the keys once you're processed." "Is that okay?"

"Yeah, thank you."

Then I rolled up my windows and stepped out of the vehicle, where I would become the property of the state of Georgia for more than six months.

My mom said God continues to present us with the same test until we finally pass it. Well, it seemed I would remain in school longer than needed. I felt entitled and wanted things as fast as I thought of them. So, without considering the long-term effects of my actions, I spent a lot of time and energy backing myself into legal and financial corners through a series of bad decisions. I also told myself it was for my kids' well-being, as justification. I wasn't afraid of hard work, because I kept a legit position.; the thrill of it all, mixed with greed, was what landed me in trouble. Plain and simple. Except the "all" sometimes included police and jail. In the end, long after the clothes I stole were "out of style," long after I had foreclosed on my home and voluntarily turned in my car, I would still be paying for crimes that had created more problems than the ones they were supposed to solve.

By the time I got my official sentence, I had sat in jail for nearly four months. My first offender's status had been revoked, and I had to sit until my trial. The charge filed by the retailer I once worked for was theft by taking. It was another felony because of the cost of the ring ($1899). The ring was the only evidence they had, but it was enough. My revised sentence was 60 days in the Atlanta Diversion Center. In the diversion center, I would be allowed daily passes to go to work, and I could drive myself back and forth, which was a big deal, seeing that I was a newly licensed Realtor and driving could prove necessary. I had passed my real estate exam a few months before buying my house. In hindsight, I was always living a double life, to the detriment of the legitimate one. As my sentence was read, I sighed with relief; *that was not so bad.* But as soon as the judge got done with my sentence, the DA commented that the diversion center had no beds available, and I might have to serve my 60 days at a detention center or wait until a bed became available. I didn't know the difference between diversion and detention at that point. I just heard 60 days and started planning my return to a normal life. I would soon be enlightened on the difference between the two.

I waited for over two weeks after court with no updates. I called my attorney, wrote to the judge, and bugged anyone that answered the phone about being transferred to the diversion/detention center. Jail was horrible, the days consisted of nasty food, metal beds with one-inch-thin mattresses, thin scratchy covers, shared county clothes down to the underwear, playing cards, reading, fighting over the phone, fighting over the television, fighting in general, and a lot of crying. The facilities were overcrowded and dirty. People were being ushered in in droves. Murderers, drug addicts, prostitutes, child abusers, traffic violators, probation violators, shoplifters, and all. Thank God I never had a problem with anyone; I just read and slept a lot. That was the best solution to stay out of trouble. They gave out extra time or solitary like commissary. Every day was filled with different drama: notes being passed between pods, people coming back from court with long ass sentences or continuance because their attorney did not show, as I said, lots of crying. What a circus.

One morning, around 3:00 a.m., unlocking my cell door woke my Bunkie and me. The system typically transfers prisoners from one place to another in the middle of the night for security reasons. I was so excited to get the hell out of Cobb County. Me and the other young lady being transferred were shackled with our hands in front, and our feet chained together. We drove for hours; I kept asking myself, *"Where are they taking me"? "My papers say Atlanta."* Finally, as the sun started rising in Georgia's backwoods, we arrived at our destination. More than 150 miles from Atlanta to Washington State Prison, Davisboro County, GA. "WTF?" When the car stopped, a hard-faced woman came over and started yelling at us like we had just enlisted in the Army. She confirmed our identities, and when I responded to my name, she caught a glimpse of my braces. Then she said, "Ms. Ellison, you can't have those braces in my place. But don't worry; our dentist will take care of that for you"."

I started to explain how this was all a mistake, that I was in the wrong place; as I nodded to my bag to indicate my sentencing papers would clear this up, she screamed at the top of her voice, "You don't speak unless permission is granted!" My eyes got bigger than her attitude as I held back tears and profanity.

Our restraints were removed, so I raised my hand to ask, "How does one get permission?" but she ignored me, turned away, and pointed to a building further up the walkway.

When we started to walk, she stopped and ordered us to march to her cadence: "Left, left, left, right, left." We fell into step, and my new normal began. They took our fingerprints and so many pictures I thought I was in a photoshoot. As soon as I was processed and assigned a bunk, I made the necessary phone calls. The first was to my parents, and the second was to my worthless-ass attorney, who had stopped taking my calls after my sentencing. Before making any more calls, I was instructed to get off the phone for headcount. After the headcount, I went to the officers' station to get my paperwork and ask a few questions. I was ignored and told to get in line behind the others.

Then we each listened to our charges, the ground rules, what constituted a violation (which was every damn thing), how you could get sent to the hole, how time could be added to our sentence, and the big one, what to do to end up across the lawn... the actual prison. I was in bootcamp, yes bootcamp, like the ones frustrated parents send their teenagers to on Maury Povich. When she got to my name, she said and I quote, "Fatou Ellison...12 months," and moved on to the next name like she was calling out Bingo numbers. I felt my knees buckle as things had just worsened for me. My palms began to sweat, and my chest tightened from the anxiety attack I was having. I patiently waited until she was done with everyone and then asked permission to approach and speak. She took her time to acknowledge me (deliberate disrespect). I had murdered many people in my dreams since that fateful night over four months ago; the amount of bullshit and discord for people in a place like this was enough to make a bitch snap. She finally said I could approach her, and I politely explained my concerns. I showed her my paperwork, and she advised me to contact my attorney and the judge to get it straightened out. Oh! I am way ahead of you. I asked for paper and a pen and sat down to start my petition for justice. While writing, I decided to pen a letter to the Georgia Bar Association to report my money-hungry, shitty-service giving lawyer.

There was a work schedule in Bootcamp, and they did not play. In bootcamp, it was early to bed and early to rise. The state saw detention as a privilege, and if you didn't see it that way, they would gladly change your mind by adding more time to your sentence. I did what I was told and won motherfuckers over with charm. I knew how to get favoritism amongst the guards. So, I could work out, go to meetings and the library, and get extra cake in the cafeteria. This may sound insignificant, but when you have been stripped of everything, all that's left is how others perceive you. This can work for or against you. I made it work for me. Well, sort of work from me. We all suffered through temperatures of over 100 degrees with no fans or air conditioning, fights, punishments, hard labor, nasty bitches, insects I had never seen before, and constant humiliation from the COs. But I was successfully faking it, quiet on the outside, rage on the inside. This is where I learned to hate for the first time. Not hate like "oh, I hate when it rains," but true "maybe I belong here type of hate." I felt it develop in me like a growing embryo, and there was no "morning after" pill to abort it. I had no one person that I hated, but it was hate. I hated that the world was still spinning; people were falling in love, raising their families, advancing their careers, traveling, and sleeping in their own beds. I no longer mattered or maybe I never mattered? Life was going on just fine without me. To add insult to injury, I was scheduled to be there for 12months. I was livid.

One extremely hot afternoon, I was sitting reading in my cell when I heard my name being called. It was the same officer that initially informed me I would be at the detention camp for 12 months. When I got to her, she handed me a letter; it was a revised sentence reflecting the original time I was given of 60 days. When I looked at the bottom of the letter and saw my release date, tears welled in my eyes. Even though I had to go to battle to get my sentence corrected, this victory gave me a needed win of sorts. After my calls and letters to the judge and the DA's office, the county forwarded the correct information to the camp. My sentence was updated in the system for a release date of less than 50 more days as opposed to the remaining 353 days quoted when I arrived. The mission was to stay out of trouble and prepare to re-enter society; easier said than done. Like the previous twelve days, the upcoming 48 would be mentally challenging, physically draining, and an emotional roller coaster. I understood the purpose of that treatment was to ensure you didn't come back, and I swore I never would. Throughout my time behind bars, I saw human beings at their worst, both inmates and guards. Based on what I saw on the inside, the family was under attack because now, more than ever, women were headed off to prison just as quickly as men. Orange had become the new black well before the Netflix original series. According to a report by the *Guardian* in 2016, women in jails were the fastest-growing incarcerated population. It further stated, "Many women leave jail with diminished prospects for physical and behavioral health recovery, with greater parental stress and strain, and even more financially precarious than before becoming caught up in the justice system." About 80% of the women in jails have dependent children The report noted that the fees and fines attached to criminal justice proceedings could have a long-term detriment to these households' financial and physical well-being. In a lot of these cases, the mother is a single mother. In a nutshell, the system was designed to be a revolving door. I had more confidence than most and I had a support system. Many did not.

The problem: that you are never finished "doing time in America." Being a convicted felon, is the American gift that keeps on giving. Shit! after the fines, fees, restitution, losing the right to vote or to bear arms, the initial loss of freedom, and missed opportunities to better oneself because of the title "felon," the "doing time" part far extends past the release date. It is funny; this same legal system allows financial criminals and certain offenders to start fresh every seven years or sooner through bankruptcy but provides little to no relief for crimes deemed unforgivable. Interesting?

Upon my release from Washington State, I took the long 158mile ride back to Marietta, GA. My parents and daughters had driven down the day before my release and stayed at my place waiting to pick me up from Cobb County Detention Center.

My dad was waiting for me in the parking lot. He smiled when he saw me, and I speed-walked the rest of the way to the car. I fell into my dad's arms and hugged him so tight. No words were spoken about the past six months on the ride home, and I was grateful for that. My mom and daughters were waiting outside for me when we pulled up to my house. My kids ran up and hugged me around the legs and waist as I fell into my mom's arms and started to weep. I remember Laila asking, "Paw, why is she crying?"

He replied, "Umm ... only your mama can answer that."

I stayed up late after the girls were put to bed. I gave my parents an overview of my sins as we sat at my kitchen table sipping Dunkin Donuts coffee. Two days later, I started feeling like myself, my dad took me to get my hair done, and I had taken more baths than needed. I went in and out of thresholds without asking permission and did not have to stand for count before I went to bed or at the break of dawn. Oh! The things I took for granted. My parents and the girls stayed for four days before returning to St. Louis. Again, my parents gave me a little time to get a vehicle, find employment and get my life in order. My village. How can I ever repay them? As hard as the road ahead was going to be, I could not imagine the countless women who had no support, no place to call home, nothing. But for me and my boatload of responsibilities, it was time to get to work. I had a mortgage to maintain (my dad brought the mortgage current after my release), I needed a vehicle (I turned mine in while incarcerated), and I needed a job. I was too new in the real estate game for that to be my bread and butter, so I put my career as a realtor on hold and sought a more reliable income.

HBO and ABC can make as many series as they want about prison. But incarceration is a BITCH, and there is nothing sexy about it. But it does provide plenty of time to reflect on everything. I lost meaning along the way because the road of the righteous was less glamorous and mundane, As I matured and became less self-centered, I started to see the lack of self-worth, depression, self-loathing, and condemnation that those choices revealed. The lesson learned: easy come, easy go.

Even with a record, I found myself in two full-time positions. One was at a small call center where we handled military calls out of Okinawa, Japan. At this company, I met two people who would become permanent fixtures in my life. During the day, I worked in a primary care physician's office, where I found a cure for my anxiety attacks. For the better part of four months, Monday–Friday, I worked at the doctor's office from 8:30 a.m.– 5:00 p.m., drive home approximately 45 minutes, fell into bed, got up, and shower left out for work at 10:30 p.m., arrive at the call center at 11:00 p.m., get off work at 7:00 a.m., drove 15 minutes to the doctor's office, slept in the car for 45 minutes, freshen up in the restroom at 8:15 a.m., then repeat. My night position was six nights a week, thus Sunday was the only day I got eight hours of sleep. When I got off at 7:00 a.m. on Sunday, I would rush home and fall into bed until nightfall. No time for men, drinks, parties, socializing ... nothing but the grind. I was in rescue mode, and I should have stayed in it.

FREE. NOT FREE

Robin was from Mobile, AL. We worked overnight together at the call center and soon became thick as thieves. The bond that tied us was our love of a good time, and for the next few years, we would travel and wreak havoc everywhere we went and with everyone. Robin lived with her police officer boyfriend. She had an eye for interior design and was a social butterfly. She was easy to be around, and I cared for her like a sister. Robin and her guy became my extended family, as we all loved to party. We even started a yearly trip to the Super Bowl, and New Orleans for the Essence Jazz Festival held every July Fourth.

One trip to the Essence Festival stands out from all the others. For those who do not know, the Essence Jazz Festival is an annual music event held in New Orleans LA, that features concerts by A list artist, celebrity hosted parties, breakout room interactions and much more. This particular year Robin and I attended multiple concerts held at the Superdome and wrapped the evening up at a Magic Johnson-sponsored after-party. Held in one of the Hilton's grand ballrooms, it was packed to capacity. There were ball players and beautiful women as far as the eyes could see. It was almost midnight when we arrived, and our consumption of an entire fifth of Hennessy was starting to get the best of us. Not like that would stop us from accepting another beverage or two.

Somehow Robin and I got separated, and my cell phone died. I became irritated because I was drunk and hungry, and my feet hurt. I searched the entire ballroom twice, but no sign of Robin. Finally, I went downstairs to the lobby to use their phone to call her ... it went straight to voicemail. I felt myself slipping into the abyss of a blackout, but I had to fight it. I started checking random hotel floors and yelling for her in empty and not-so-empty bathrooms, but still no Robin. The Hilton had over 23 floors, and after about an hour, I started to panic. I also had to use the restroom, so I stumbled into the next bathroom I came to. As soon as I pushed the door open, who did I see? Robin. Sitting on a sink ledge, having a heart-to-heart with some random dude in the ladies' bathroom.

I was like, "What the fuck, Robin? How could you leave me? I've been looking all over for you!" She was screaming the same thing at me. We both looked confused, like who left who? I went into a stall to pee while Robin and her mystery guy tried to argue their case on how we got separated. Unconvinced, I reached under the bathroom door to gesture my feelings about the situation. After I relieved myself and washed my hands, I told Robin I was ready to go. She asked for a few more minutes and said she would meet me in the lobby. I agreed and left the restroom. The party was breaking up, and the elevators and escalators were overcrowded. I had been in heels all day, so I took my shoes off. Probably not the most sanitary thing to do, but I had no choice. Thirty minutes later, I made it to the lobby. On the way, I was approached by several men making unsuccessful attempts to get into my good graces or maybe just my goods. I waited for Robin; I went back up to the restroom she was in ... no Robin.

Everything from this point on was a blur. I vaguely recall a man approaching me to assist with putting my shoes back on. I believe I was outside because he said, "Oh baby girl, put your shoes on; you don't want to get glass in those pretty feet, do you? "Let's get these back on." The next thing I remember is a faint knocking on a door. My eyes slowly opened as a lady's voice was saying something, but I was still foggy and couldn't comprehend anything. Just like when I woke up on the side of 285, it took me a minute to come to my senses.

She knocked again, and as I heard the word "Housekeeping," I yelled out, "Hold on!" but the words were not mine. Then I heard it again as I hurried to the door; I stopped in my tracks and turned my head towards the sound of the voice as I mimicked reaching for the door. Two men were in the room with me, and I slept in the bed with one of them. The fear must have shown on my face as both men were now awake and talking so fast, I almost threw up. I did a quick body check and noticed I was fully dressed and that I had slept on top of the comforter and my bedmate slept underneath. I made these observations as I opened the door to the room for housekeeping, still trying to make out what the men were saying. The housekeeper was just as confused and did not know whether to stay or leave. Finally, one of the men asked housekeeping to come back shortly as another gentleman walked in pass her with coffees on a tray. I was still standing by the door, not saying a word. They recounted how I was drunk, barefoot, had lost my friend, and couldn't remember what hotel I was staying in. I had given them Robin's number, but their calls went straight to voicemail. As frightened as I was about what could have happened to me, the look on these guys' faces showed they were just as frightened. Now, they were not sure they had made the right decision to help a damsel in distress or a barefoot drunk.

Still at the front door. Everyone was assuring me of their innocence from the night before. I was scared but blessed to be alive. One of the men called Robin to see if she would answer; she finally did and gave them our hotel information. I breathed for the first time in what felt like an hour. I whispered, "thank you," and gathered my things. On the way to my hotel, I was scolded and warned about the dangers of what could have happened the previous night. The guy who drove me stopped and got breakfast for me, him, and Robin.

When we finally arrived at my hotel, I could tell Robin had not slept, and she was pacing back and forth, threatening to murder me before I allowed someone else to. She and the guy took turns, and rightfully so, about how dangerous, and reckless I had been. Before leaving, he kissed my cheeks and said he would like to see me again. He reached into his pocket, retrieved his business card, and said, "How about tonight? I'll have two tickets at will call for you ladies." He took our names and instructed us to be there no later than the show's second half. After he left, I showered and passed out. When we arrived at the Superdome, I called him, and he met us at will call, still a gentleman. After getting our tickets, he had us follow him to our seats. Right next to the stage with backstage access! Robin and I looked at each other and did a silent scream. The men who saved my ass the night before were the band members of the closing act to the Essence Festival that year. Our seats were unbelievable. We drank, mostly water for me, danced, and sang at the top of our voices as we had one of the most surprising ends to what could have been a horrible excursion. Upfront and personal with a legend. Adios, New Orleans!

Robin and I drove in silence most of the way back to Atlanta. I reflected on the events of the weekend and shook my head. God watches over babies and fools. Although I tell this story lightly, the fear I felt standing in that room with those men, having awakened from a slumber that gave me no rest, would stay with me forever.

I made some life adjustments when I got back to Atlanta. I left both the doctor's office and call center for a better opportunity. I started another position at the encouragement of Thomas, the other person I met at the call center. The new gig was like the one we had overnight, but with better pay and regular hours. With that regular schedule, my daughters could move back with me and resume their life in Atlanta. The things people do not tell you about getting out of jail after any amount of time is how long it can take to get financially stable. Jeez. I figured it would take me a couple of months, but it was the better part of a year, and things were still tight. To help bridge the gap, I started a side hustle. I researched a couple of options and settled on one. After, registering the business, creating a logo, and getting a merchant account and an 800 number, and choosing a name, I started my escort service. Before you judge, it was really a no brainer for me. The thought of having powerful and influential people partake in the forbidden world of paying for ... companionship.

Several nights a week, I would peruse the clubs to pass out cards with my female friends (bait) to see which fish were biting. About two weeks into it, I got my first big referral. It was the most anticipated athletes in Atlanta sports in decades. When I got the call, I felt like the Mayflower Madam or Heidi Fleiss. I needed this service to be extraordinary so that I could build my empire one player at a time. Since I was the boss, I went on the first few calls (especially this one) to ensure safety, introduce myself and get my money—$2000 for a conversation between my athlete and two of my girls for one hour. After that, I started to do the math and, just like the money order scheme, I got tunnel vision. The big client came so easy, so I took for granted that it always would. I focused on creating an experience for each client; it was my job to acquire, develop and manage my team to deliver. Using my interpersonal skills and ability to convey the bigger picture, it was relatively easy to find ready, willing, and able ladies. There were no cons, lies, or deception, just a clearly defined message. "You are always in control until you choose not to be. Be professional, be quiet, be attentive, be sexy, be discreet." Get paid.

Most of the women agreed to the terms for one reason, quick money. 60 minutes could easily turn into 20 minutes for the same pay. I became consumed with scaling, and Robin was my right-hand man. Which was my first mistake. Mixing business and friends can be a recipe for disaster. Robin was cool but lacked the necessary focus, and I wanted to get things done and run a cohesive, successful escort service. But how?

In the long run, I started spending more time dealing with people's poor work ethics than booking clients. I was working my fulltime job, taking care of my family, and now babysitting grown-ass women walking away with more in 2 hours than they made in a week on their day jobs. After a few "no-show" calls from clients, I was over it. I did not trust anyone, so a no-show was a red flag for me. Yeah, I wanted to make money, but I could only do that with happy clients. There's no telling what a disgruntled person might have done, and I was not staying around to find out. Additionally, the "no-shows" made me think side deals were being made, and I did not have the bandwidth to monitor that on to the next!

Back at square one, my only income was my day job, but I needed more, to make up for lost wages. To make mattes more dire, the company I worked for was involved in a historical financial scandal. which put my stable income in jeopardy Customers were threatening us and canceling their service in droves. The decrease in income made it unjustifiable to continue my hour and a half each way commute. I thought hard and long about giving real estate another shot. I had two kids and a mortgage and a requirement to do things legally. I thought about giving real estate another shot. After all, I was incarcerated shortly after passing my exam and signing on with a brokerage. I didn't get the opportunity to fully commit to it. The first broker I signed with was the worst. There were no systems in place, no training, and no mentorship. On my first day, a fellow agent gave me a newspaper and a script and told me to start dialing. WTF? That experience put a sour taste in my mouth regarding a career in real estate. But with few options, I decided to give it another try.

More than two years had passed since I've gotten my real estate license. Unfortunately, I had not completed my continuing education, and my license lapsed. I ordered an online course and started all over again. The self-study proved challenging, and it took me three tries to pass the state exam, but I passed. The following business day, after passing, I began interviewing with companies and found a home with a nationally recognized brokerage. The people, the training, the education, and the business model were something I had never experienced. I dressed the part, spoke the language, and was a quick study because of my past mortgage experience. I worked late and came in early. Real estate is where I got my first real taste of workplace diversity. The thing about money, it is a universal language, and I was fluent. I knew my numbers. When I brought a mock HUD 1 to a potential client's home during a listing interview, they could compare it with the actual closing HUD 1 later and get within 2% of my calculations. I was afraid to prospect the million-dollar listings, but I ate where I got an opportunity to shine with homes that ranged from $179k to $389k. As the head of my household, working on commission only was scary, but every presentation got me that much closer to a signed agreement, which led to a contract, ultimately leading to a closing and, finally, a payday. I was learning and mingling with different people and having the time of my life. Real Estate was the new man in my life, and I was head over heels in love.

MY NEW LOVE

A couple of years after entering the world of residential real estate, I met Teddy James. Teddy was a close friend of my hair stylist. He was always at the beauty shop when I went to my appointments plus he seemed cool. We always talked about real estate and investments. Within months of us meeting, Teddy was sitting for his real estate exam. Once he got his license, he signed on with the same broker I worked for (at a different location). By this time, we had become close friends. I hung out with him and his fiancée, and he and I eventually went into business together. We formed an LLC to purchase and sell the properties we acquired. The best thing about this partnership is that we each brought value to it. Teddy once owned a car lot back in New York, so he was a good negotiator and savvied with his money.

On the other hand, I had great interpersonal skills and a work ethic unrivaled by most. Flipping houses had challenges, but overall, we were a kick-butt team. We perused the foreclosure list, put up "we buy houses" signs, and worked around the clock. Teddy and I were on a quest to be the best flippers in our area. Privately, I was on a mission to prove I had changed for the better.

Before our business collaboration, I had a tough year. Even after all my efforts to stay afloat, I still foreclosed on my home. The girls went to St. Louis again until I got back on my feet, and I moved in with one of my girlfriends and her mom. I was at rock bottom financially, but my spirits were high. I loved everything about real estate and could not wait to get a y place again and bring the girls back home. I was running on emotional fumes, missing my daughters, our home, our life together. Teddy had other reasons, his wedding was quickly approaching, and the responsibilities of having a wife as opposed to a live-in girlfriend made him push harder. Nothing happened overnight, but we made solid investment deals with diligence and honesty.

We were a great team, but there was a darkness lurking that I neglected to address until it addressed me. I worked hard and played hard. However, I was single with no one at home to attend to. I dated multiple people for fun, but nothing serious. My dating caused awkwardness between Teddy and me. I looked to him for advice in business and admired his relationship with his fiancée. I considered him family and valued his opinion. When I finally connection with a companion Teddy was more than vocal about how he felt. He would say things like, "Be careful," or, "He doesn't sound serious about you!" He would also pry to see if we had slept together. His attitude and negative feedback were a cause for pause. I stopped disclosing my personal business with Teddy and kept the focus on our business goals. I was never naïve about what Teddy's protest about my dating meant, but I just shook it off. He was my male perspective, so I kept an open mind.

Glenn was tall, dark, handsome, professional, and well-spoken. To sum it up, he was what I needed. Great conversation, funny and engaging. We saw each other often. We were not intimate, and I preferred to keep it that way. I had reservations about getting into a physical relationship while emotionally dealing with so much. I was totally happy with what we had. He provided a distraction from all the noise in my head. After my foreclosure and sending the girls back to St. Louis, I isolated myself for more than six months from everyone except my roommate and work. He was a breath of fresh air. Glenn gave me a healthy adult relationship without talking about my past. But he would only get so far.

Glenn was the right guy at the wrong time. Deep inside, I had my guard up and felt too unstable to get involved romantically. Maybe I missed out, but I had this idea that I could only love wholeheartedly once all my pieces had come together. I knew the type of man I could settle down with, but I had not yet become the woman for that man. Of course, he eventually wanted more, and his one-way hour-long commutes were taking its toll. Plus, my schedule was not one of leisure. I had a lot of ground to make up. It did not help that Teddy was always scheduling meetings with homeowners or events for us to attend. Whenever we wrapped up for the day, Teddy would inquire about my evening plans with Glenn or whomever. I sensed his jealousy, but I never felt like confronting him. This I would regret.

One evening, after a long day at work and going out for drinks, Teddy asked if he could sober up at my place before hitting the road. After about an hour, I asked him to call his fiancée Kenya, and let her decide whether he should sleep on my couch, drive home or if she could pick him up. Then, I started prepping for bed while he stumbled around the living room. I called out from my room to see what Kenya said, but he did not answer. I walked into the living room to see if he had fallen back asleep, but he was wide awake. He startled me when he finally said. "Faye," with a long pause.

"Huh?"

He repeated, "FAYE!" before he could say anything else to make that moment more awkward, I grabbed his coat and escorted his ass to the door. When he got in his truck, I stood in the darkness for a moment and replayed the evening. My phone ringing caught me by surprise, and his voice on the other end spoke words that should have changed the relationship. I was more than irritated by Teddy's sexual suggestions for many reasons, but I shook it off. The next day, he called to apologize for his behavior and blamed it on the alcohol. I accepted his apology because I needed to move forward in our business endeavors and not stay stuck on his inappropriateness. We were still friends and business partners but now with limitations.

Fast forward two months, Teddy, and his fiancée, were set to marry in his native Jamaica. It was 2003, and many of his and her friends and family were to embark on a four-day, three-night getaway to help the happy couple make it official. Throughout the mini vacation, we enjoyed exquisite cuisine, great company, beautiful weather, relaxation, the beach, Dunn's River, and more. The wedding party decided to go out the night before the wedding. Since we were guests of the groom, Robin and I spent most of our time with the groom's party. We took over Kingston like a plague. Our party hit the adult entertainment scene, bars, and all the nightlife Kingston had to offer.

At our last stop, everyone met up on the dance floor. One of the groomsmen and I were dancing and enjoying each other's company. more than most. We snuck off to the men's room when no one was looking. Yes, the men's room; before we could close the door to our bathroom stall, guess who came pushing through like he was busting his 16-year-old daughter on prom night? Teddy. After we demanded that he get lost and go be with his wife, we abandoned our attempt to get physical, left the bathroom, and returned to the dance floor.

Soon after, we call it a night and headed back to the resort. The wedding was scheduled for the late afternoon the following day, so we still had plenty of time to hang out before shutting it down for the night. Everyone ended up in one of the groomsmen's rooms. Some of the guys and Robin started a game of spades, and someone else rolled a blunt and started passing it around. Raymond, the grooms-man from the club's bathroom, and I retreated to the balcony to talk. At some point, I excused myself to use the restroom. When I walked through the room, I noticed Robin and another groomsman had disappeared. I kind of giggled to myself and proceeded to the restroom. I rejoined Raymond on the balcony, and shortly after, Teddy came out and asked to see Raymond, he excused himself, and I sat on the balcony talking in the picturesque view. After about twenty minutes, I went in to check on him. When I walked into the room, everyone except

Teddy was gone. I recalled the guys talking about going downstairs to the pool and a late-night bar. I mentioned it briefly and said I was going downstairs to join them.

As I started towards the door, a loud knock startled me. Teddy grabbed my arm and put his index finger towards his lips to signal silence. I had no idea why I should have been quiet until he said in a panic, "Oh shit! It's Kenya!" Still no cause for concern on my part, but before I knew it, I was being escorted into the bathroom, unable to make heads or tails of exactly what was happening and why he was in the bathroom with me. Before I could protest his company, Teddy was on me like a madman. He was on his knees and under my dress before I could blink my eyes. It took me a moment to get my bearings as he attempted to pull my legs apart. This small-ass bathroom did not provide enough space for consensual sex, let alone a struggle. As I pushed and pried his hands and face away from me, it was like wrestling with an octopus. He was determined for me to give in. I was determined not to puke. I kept telling myself that this was all a misunderstanding, and I was more fucked up than I thought. But it wasn't, and that was happening. Finally, I managed to get out of the bathroom. as Teddy seemingly managed to keep from falling in the tub. I got a good push-in and went for the bedroom door. Teddy grabbed me from behind and slammed me onto the bed. I am quite strong, so I had no idea why I did not just elbow this nigga in the face. Where was my strength? Why couldn't I get my thoughts together? But the "just get through this" persona I had developed all those years back with Daryl started to eclipse me. I could feel my soul leave the room as his verbiage became unbearable.

My head began to swim as I felt myself began to black out. The baby doll-length dress I wore made it easier for him to violate me. I was in a battle and losing. I kept repeating, "You don't have to do this," then more aggressively, "Get the fuck off me!" My self-worth dropped quicker than Enron's stock value after its' public scandal. I fought to stay conscious, but I wanted no memory of this to add to the laundry list of things I had to overcome. I kept thinking, *where is everyone?* Then, just as I felt my body succumbing to all the alcohol and marijuana I enjoyed throughout the evening, I got a glimpse of the person I thought was my friend.

On top of me as if we were on our honeymoon. Disrespecting me as a woman, a mother, a business partner, and a person. Putting his selfish desires in the space where trust once resided. The look on his face made me sick to my stomach, I felt vomit forming in my throat but fought to hold it in. As I fought back slipping into unconsciousness, I wondered how long my friend had been a rapist. How many others were there? I wondered who else knew what his intentions were that night. The one thing I never wondered about again was our future. This was his end game, and he chose another country to carry out his demonic plans. I am the thing he had planned for his prewedding day jitters. Teddy actions said, "Fuck you, Faye," while fucking me. It was the exclamation point to end our friendship. The next day he would be a married man, and I would be suicidal.

These thoughts enraged me, and with a burst of energy, I smacked Teddy so hard he jerked backward, which allowed me to get my leg under his stomach to kick him halfway across the room. I walked to the door and straightened my clothes. I was humiliated and disgusted. When I got to my room, Robin and her male friend were there. When they saw me, both jumped to their feet and, in unison, asked, "What's happened?"

I just wanted to shower and pause until daybreak, but the words came out like that vomit almost did a few minutes earlier. "Teddy had sex with me!" I couldn't even say the word rape.

To this, they both responded, "Wait, what?" Robin was so confused she said, "Like did you want to or did he, you know, take it?" obviously, she could not say the word either.

But Robert, the groomsman said it. "Like raped you?" Once those words were spoken, it was as if the assault happened again. Then Robin pointed to the open balcony door and the next room where the bride-to-be was getting her beauty rest. Wow! His fiancée was less than 50 feet from the woman her soon-to-be husband had violated in the worst way imaginable. I was further devastated by Robin's reaction. I had shared a horrible detail with her, and she was more concerned with the bride hearing about it than seeing that I was okay. It seemed as if Robin was confused, I started to repeat myself, but was interrupted by a loud knock on our door. Her reaction hinted to the possibility that I was dealing with a woman who may have chosen silence after her own life experience.

Things started to escalate once Teddy got into our room. Robert, who was in the room with Robin, was still frozen from my initial declaration. He kept asking me if I was okay or if I needed help. As soon as he saw Teddy, he grabbed him. "What the fuck did you do, man?" he said while escorting him back out the door. He even stated that I had every right to tell Kenya what happened. I stood in silence as Robert and Robin gave Teddy the same warning about his future wife's proximity as Robin had given me. He kept fighting Robert, trying to get back into our room while screaming that he was sorry. He was not begging for forgiveness; he was pleading for me to remain silent. He did not give a fuck about me.

I wanted to forget about everything. I didn't want this to be my life. *What a bitch;* I thought Teddy was so self-assured that I would not involve the authorities that all he thought about was his fiancée finding out. I hated Teddy and God at that moment, but above all else, I hated myself. What about me gave Teddy the green light to shatter more pieces of my fragile existence? For the next couple of hours, Robert and Robin came and went; the phone kept ringing, someone kept knocking on the door, and the commotion kept me awake. I showered, crawled under the covers, and waited. I waited for the numbness to wear off; I waited for morning, hoping this was all a nightmare. When Robin finally lay down, the bedroom fell silent. Besides the occasional sniffles of our quiet cries, we never discussed that night for the remainder of the trip.

"Our minds are not designed to do things that are difficult, scary or uncertain." *Mel Robbins*.

I NEED A MINUTE

I pondered long and hard about going to the local police or at least security at the resort. I struggle with my inner thoughts. *Would people believe I led him on? Would they speak about how close we were? How I interacted with his friend? Or would they say I was upset because he was getting married?* Would people use my past against me? My flirtatious disposition, my many lovers, my criminal record, the foreclosure, and the abortions; I could be made out to look like a vindictive slut instead of a woman partaking in her friend's wedding festivities. And that was that. Once again, I chose the path of least resistance...silence. I was a coward, a person who lacked courage. And this time, Teddy was the victorious one. The look on his face when he violated me haunted me all night. As I finally fell asleep, I accepted that I would have to bear this cross alone. The next day, I attended the wedding and returned to my room, and for the third time in my life, contemplated murder, and my suicide.

Back in the States, I could not function properly; I felt sick and anxious, shame and angry. The thought of Teddy's disgusting touch made my body quiver. Most of the time, I felt like a piece of shit as I tried to move throughout my day. Finally, I did what I was used to, doing by silencing my thoughts; I picked up some childhood companions to join me in my recovery (vodka, rum, and tequila). I had been a target of a hate crime, and I could not shake the aftermath. Since those shots of whatever my cousin made me drink at the tender age of nine, alcohol had become part of my healing process. After my Jamaica ordeal, it became increasingly necessary.

One evening, some friends and I went out for dinner and drinks. On my way home, I stopped at a Quick Trip to grab some snacks. About a mile down the road, blue and white lights hit my rearview mirror. I did not think anything of it, so I pulled over and turned off my engine. "Ma'am, I pulled you over because you were not maintaining your lane," was how the officer greeted me. "Have you been drinking?"

"No sir," was my answer.

"Do you mind stepping out of the car?" I was like, "For what?"

"I smell alcohol; please step out of your vehicle."

I thought nothing of it. I was confident the drinks I had hours ago were no longer in my system. So, like a dummy, I started those stupid-ass sobriety tests. Ten minutes later, I was in handcuffs and being ushered into the back of a police vehicle. At one thirty in the morning, about four miles from home, I was getting locked up while everyone else I was with earlier was probably on their way to sleep. After I was processed and taken to population, I passed out on the paper-thin mattress and fell asleep.

Later that morning, I called my roommate and informed her of my whereabouts. I stayed locked up for three days before I was released. I was still on probation from my six-month stint at Washington State, so I had to get approval from my PO to be released. When I got home, my friend's mom wanted to have a heart-to-heart with me. She was crying and saying she wanted to be there for me and that I could talk to her about anything. I felt immensely touched and embarrassed. I was not in the mood to disclose my background to anyone, especially the who, what, when, where, how, and particularly the whys. I avoided telling pertinent information that evening and made plans to hasten my exit. Even though my friend and her mom were authentic, and our co-habitation was easy, I needed my own space. The house was no longer large enough to accommodate the three of us and my past.

Teddy and I sold a couple of properties we owned collectively, and I signed over the remaining one and dissolved our LLC. I manage to get this done with minimal to no interaction with him. That proceeds from those sells allowed me to move out of my friends home quicker than originally planned. Although legally, my life was in shambles, my professional life was thriving. I was able to obtain two properties in a blue-ribbon school district. I moved into one and rented the other out. One of the properties came from a lady who lost her job and wanted to keep her credit intact. The other came from prospecting the expired home listing through FMLS. As luck would have it, one of the sellers I spoke with was having trouble selling her father's home. He had passed the year before, and she could not continue taking care of his estate and her own. I scheduled an appointment to meet with her, and ultimately moved into that home. A beautiful two-story, stucco, on a full basement in a middle-upper-class subdivision. This was long overdue. It was time to put some wins back in my column. My daughters moved back home, and life was good. We loved our community, and I loved what I did for a living. Real estate gave me a focus like nothing else had, it also gave me the flexibility to volunteer at the girls' schools, participate in their activities and be present. It was like. well, normal. I managed to run my household, prepare three meals a day, help with homework and school projects, keep a clean orderly home, take the girls to tutoring, ballet, chorus, gymnastics, school plays, vacations, party, get DUI's, live on probation, and sell beautiful home to my clients. That was my normal.

Patterns and habits can be challenging to change. My real estate family was just that, family. Through my five years at Coldwell Banker, my colleagues and I supported each other through fundraisers, events, ground-breaking ceremonies, open houses, weddings, funerals, births, and parties. One of those parties landed me back in hot water. (patterns) It was my co-worker's husband's birthday bash. A Caribbean themed party where the rum punch really provided a punch. The event was held quite a distance from where I lived, but that never stopped me before. I had a couple of drinks or more and a bite to eat, not realizing how the rum punch affected me until it was time to go; I stumbled out of the party around 2:00 a.m. A gentleman I was conversing with throughout the night escorted me to my car, and he was adamite about not letting me drive. But I won that argument by promising to stop for coffee and notify him when I arrived home. I sat in my car for a few minutes before pulling off. Unfamiliar with the area and with no Google maps to steer me in the right direction, I drove around for what seemed like an eternity looking for the interstate. By the time I found the on ramp, I dozed off at the red light that preceded my left turn onto the interstate. A tap on my window awakened me. It was a state police officer. He asked me if I was okay, to which I replied,

"Yup." He then asked if I had been drinking, to which I replied, "Nope." he asked me if I needed to step out for some fresh air. I did not answer.

"Ma'am, I'm here because someone called to report a woman asleep in her car at the light." "I believe that's you."

By this point, I was irritated and just wanted to be left alone. He asked me to step out of my vehicle again. This time it was not a suggestion, so I exited the car and gave the worst sobriety results he had ever seen. Months later, when my court date rolled around, the judge and a packed courtroom looked at me in disbelief as the details of my traffic stop were read aloud. I was violent, super drunk, belligerent, and insisted on going home. With each word he read, I began to shrink. In all, for the two cases, I spent a total of five nights in jail, paid fees/fines of $3000, which included my attorney cost, and was ordered to make monthly payments to have a breathalyzer installed in my vehicle for 60 days. And that was getting off easy. Legal shenanigans.

FEELING EXHILARATED

"In the beginning, God created the heavens and the earth. The earth was without form and void. Simple." The words coming from the podium made me feel like I was a child back at Morning Star Baptist Church. "Then, as the days went by, beautiful creatures, water, sky, etcetera were created. Life starts without form or void and is quickly filled with experiences, judgments, interactions, surroundings, encounters, and to top it off … our interpretation of it all." I sat at the Landmark education seminar with the curiosity of a child. Being told that a meaningless life was a life of freedom and living fully self-expressed was news to me. The first time she said it, I thought *Bullshit*. Someone telling me that my life is or should be meaningless seemed disrespectful. But once she elaborated, I got it. A meaningless life is one in which we experience life as is, without adding our personal interpretation or feelings to it.. I murmured to myself as the New Zealand native speaker watched the faces in the audience as we tried to grasp what was being conveyed. I was at a self-help workshop that my real estate mentor Don had invited me to. Don and I had known each other for about three years. I guess he could see or feel my internal fight between living a life I was proud of versus one I was very much ashamed of, and this was his way of helping.

As the speaker continued to explain how God meant for us to live meaningless lives, she said void is not necessarily bad but may hold the key to inner peace. I pondered on all I had done and all the things that had been done to me. I knew no other way but to add meaning to everything. Then came my aha moment: "The things that we allow to fill the void and the meaning we add to our lives are either moving us towards our best self or working against us." I thought to myself, *Ladies, and gentlemen, I am sad to report that based on this theory, I have been working against my best self since my seventh birthday.* Throughout this introduction to the weekend-long course, there were invitations to sign up and partake in the full experience. Unfortunately, I did not join the course that night It would take me another year to register and embark on a new journey.

A year later, my life class took place over the weekend. It was a three-day, 12-hour-per-day, eye-opening training I found the work required to participate to be both personal and revealing. I learned to honor my word and be accountable for my life. I was given assignments that required me to make amends with people through phone calls and/or letters. First, I had to call people I owed an apology. Next, I was tasked with identifying inauthentic areas in my life and choose whether to remain that way or make a change. The final assignment was to invite people to my graduation whom I believed could benefit from the course. These invites; had to be personal to our story and journey. The invite would be my extension of love and forgiveness, or to ask for forgiveness.

Teddy (my ex-business partner), Robin, my dad, and my boyfriend were the people I chose to invite. When I called Teddy, whom I had not spoken to or seen since the incident in Jamaica, he picked up on the first ring. At my life-class graduation, I embraced my invitees, even Teddy. When I embraced Teddy, Robin began to cry. I wanted to stop being angry, and this program was helping me put things in perspective for the first time in my life. My boyfriend, whom I told about the Teddy situation, was not so moved. He was upset, that I had reached out and invited, the person he saw as a monster, to the ceremony. He was furious and wanted to harm Teddy. My response was, inviting Teddy demonstrated the power of awareness and forgiveness I had gained over that three-day course, and he should consider signing up as well. It was a quiet ride home.

The next night, while cooking dinner, there was a knock on my front door. The girls almost knocked me down, running to open it. They were upstairs and had caught a glimpse of the person on the other side. To my surprise, it was my dad. He was one of the calls I made to people I felt had wronged me. I was hurt that my dad did not protect me from his nephew. When I made the call a couple of days earlier, my exact words were, "Dad, I'm calling you because I'm in a training course about life, and my assignment is to call those people I have wronged or those I believed have wronged me. I am calling you because I have been harboring resentment that you were not there to protect me when I needed you. It was unfair because you were unaware, and I never came to you for help or guidance about it." He started to interrupt me, but I wouldn't let him. Those were the rules; allow space for the person we called to listen and not get into a debate. When I was done, I could feel the hurt and confusion from his end of the phone as he tried to understand what he had missed. I went further to say it did not matter why I was angry with him; I only needed to apologize and forgive him. I gave him no details about his alleged missed opportunity to protect me, and I never would.

SELF PROCLAIMED THREE-TIME LOSER

Our story began one night when I was doing a drive-by on my then boyfriend Wyatt, whom I suspected had just lied to me about his whereabouts. Wyatt and I had been through a rough spot, and trust was becoming more difficult. So, one evening, after he said he was headed to the gym, I got into my car to make sure I saw him there … alone. After getting confirmation, I proceeded home. Pulling off the lot, I noticed a handsome gentleman in a late-model Range Rover looking oh so debonaire. We caught each other's attention, and he waved me down and asked me to pull over. He exited his truck, came over, and introduced himself. I almost choked when he handed me his business card. Eric Williams, owner of Eric's grooming parlor, located a few miles down the road.

, I met up with him the following day for lunch. He was attractive, a little shorter than I liked, but his personality made up the difference. He didn't waste time going into his sales pitch, he said. "I'm 39 years old. I have five kids and one grandbaby, been married twice, did nine years, have big feet, I love cars, and getting that money." He continued, "I'm not a dough boy; my hustle is the hair business. I have two shops on Roswell Road one here in Buckhead, the other in Sandy Springs. I just thought I'd tell you who I am upfront because I don't like wasting time."

I thought to myself, *Except for those wasted years in prison,* but who was I to judge?

. To summarize our first date, I was sold on Eric before he spoke. I laughed a little because I already knew much about Eric thanks to Wyatt. Wyatt would bragged how his barber had money, cars, and was purchasing a huge estate not far from his shop in Sandy Springs. That same man, my guy, bragged about for months, was about to replace him. Later that night, when we spoke, I let Eric in on my little secret. I told him about Wyatt, to which he replied, "Well, he'll have to find a new barber, he's a decent dude, but I won't be able to cut his hair anymore."

"Really?" I asked, Eric said that Wyatt talked just as much about me to him as he did to me about Eric. He let out a laughed and commented on how small Atlanta was. He explained how he used to give Wyatt relationship advice and how crazy it was to meet the woman he once advises his client about. "Shit, based on your boy's conversations, I'll be a better fit for you than he is anyway." I chuckled because, on the surface, it seemed he was right. That Friday night, Eric and I went out to dinner and talked for hours; he was funny, honest, and attentive. The next day, I arranged lunch with Wyatt. My goal was to end the relationship—yes, leave my man for his barber—and that is exactly what I did.

"The grass is only greener on the other side because someone is watering it." Anonymous

Eric's strength was that he was attentive and analyzed people to perfection. I would later discover that this was a necessary trait for a psychopath. Eric was a fast and smooth talker; he possessed high dollar items and rubbed shoulders with the well-known and influential. But Eric had a plan and needed a certain type of woman to execute it. I believe he thought I was more financially secure than I was; I looked the part just like him. However, I was far from it, just like him. It wasn't long before I couldn't keep account of his taking and giving. I thought he had access to more cash than he did and thought I was a good girl.

Ultimately, he and I were looking for the same things in the wrong places. I wanted someone who could quarterback the life I was creating, great in bed, and impeccably dressed....so did he. I give him credit for hitting the ground running after his nine-year stint. He managed to accomplish more upon his release than some men with no criminal record. That tenacity is what I became attracted to. I could not fathom what it took to move forward after a nine-year bid with no support upon release, but he did it. We started good, like most relationships, but less than two months in, he gave me a little too much information about his life. That was the day I decided Eric would stay in the friends-with-benefits zone. He was about to go on another extended vacation. Wow! The halo effect Eric once had, vanished as he spilled his heart out about the new case pending against him. Eric's fake it 'til you make it plan was proving a problem. Although Eric was a natural salesperson, he was hell bent on spending his talent and energy on gathering worldly possession to impress people, rather than invest that time and energy into becoming a better person. He spent every waking moment convincing anyone who would listen of his plans and how much money they should invest in them. Over the next decade, I would hear about those plans a million times as we would enter and exit each other's lives like seasons. Then out of nowhere it would take one devious act for me to cut ties from Eric for good.

"Eighty-six percent of women in jails reported experiencing sexual violence at some point in their life, roughly four times the rate of women in the US at large." (Lartey, 2016)

The clothes that fit me perfectly when I was arrested were now too big for me. I had to hold my pants up as I walked through the doors to the other side of my life. My 45-day stay in the Cobb

County Adult Detention Center released me in a physical state much different than when I was booked. I had lost weight, and my lips were discolored and peeling from lack of water and moisture. The whites of my eyes were a soft yellow from dehydration, and the contacts I wore the night I got locked up were ready to crack inside my sockets. My hair was in braids, and I looked more like a child than a woman with two children of her own. From a distance, one may have thought that I had been in a physical altercation, but upon closer observation, it was obvious ... I was in a crisis. The reason behind this arrest was not much different than the prior ones. Just before midnight, exactly two miles from my house, the flashing blue lights danced in my rearview mirror. I saw the officer make a U-turn, but I had no idea he did so for me. He asked if I had been drinking before he could even get to my window; then, he asked if I was aware that my headlight was out. I answered, "No sir," to both. He then demanded I step out of the car for a sobriety check. Once I politely declined, he asked me to exit anyway and read my rights. He then asked Eric for his identification and placed him under arrest. I was in custody for refusing a sobriety test and Eric for an outstanding warrant. Not my idea of a power couple.

At the county jail, we were split up and placed in holding cells. I was awakened by the popping sound of the holding cell door opening about two hours later to stash away yet another inmate. The later it got, the crazier the people became. Crying, screaming, stinking, intoxicated, all the shit that's typical of jail life. Once again, I found my accommodations contradicting the life I betrayed on the outside. The tug of war between right and wrong had lasted longer than most religious wars, and I was losing. When the news of my arrest reached St. Louis, I was entering the general population (gen. pop). It was the summer, and my girls were in St. Louis for their regular visit.

Sidebar, I did a lot better with my girls around than without them. Too much idle time was not good for me. There was a lesson to learn from my repeat offenses, but I kept failing the test.

I kept believing I knew what, who, and where was best for me. I was proven wrong all the time. If I was going to end this pathology of going in and out of jail, I had to start doing things differently. Every day I spent behind bars, I lost years of income, influence, clarity, and self-esteem. The more I got locked up, the longer it took to return to normal upon my release. It was hard to fathom that just 45 days earlier; I was enjoying some of the fruits of my hard labor. Until a blown headlight and a few drinks, ushered in an unthinkable level of turmoil.

I had become familiar with picking up the pieces after a setback, but this time was a little more complicated. I had less than two weeks to work things out with my landlord, catch up on my bills, perform my probation duties, get the girls back and on a schedule before school started, and get my car back from Robin, who had borrowed it while I was on vacation. Those were the things I knew I had to accomplish. What I didn't know was that a strategically placed phone call to my broker would take priority over everything else. After I was arrested, I was denied bond. So, I got to work to mitigate some possible fallout within my personal and professional life, i.e. my clients. My plan was to have my cousin Darby check my message daily, and each evening I would provide her with responses and instructions on how to handle questions and requests.

Please note, I would have done that myself, but when you're in jail, there's a message that randomly comes on during your phone calls, disclosing that you are calling from a correction center. So, to avoid that, I had Darby perform that task for me. Check my voicemail, and answer my 1 call, so I can provide next steps. I need to point out that Darby volunteered to help in any way she could, so I asked the previous and scheduled a time for me to call her each evening. Point, blank, period.

The first set of calls for her to make would be to my clients, informing them of a family emergency and my uncertain return date. I assumed if my client's received communication and updates; things would remain intact. I wanted my clients to know that the marketing of their homes would continue without interruption. I further asked her to contact another agent I was close to and give her access to my clients and listings so she could answer any questions about my properties while I was away. Simple enough, right? At least, that is what I thought. But Darby's next moves were perplexing. When we planned this out, I took for granted that she was listening to me and would follow my instructions. But I was sorely mistaken. Instead of calling the numbers I had given her, Darby decided to call my broker directly. She told him that I had been in a car accident outside of Illinois and was in critical condition in a local Illinois hospital. What was she thinking? I didn't just work at the brokerage; my co-workers were my extended family for the past five years. So, once she made that call, it set in motion a chain reaction that put my livelihood and reputation in critical condition. The news of my accident spread like wildfire throughout the office. This diverse team of individuals went to work to help and ensure my speedy recovery. They pulled up Illinois state patrol and highway safety incidents, contacted my emergency contacts and called hospitals and towing companies. This took place while I sat in jail, clueless to what chaos was brewing. It can be quite difficult to re-emerge untouched when a rumor of my near death experience festered for more than a month with no word from me. People lost trust and began to doubt the person they once thought I was.

After the initial shock of Darby's mishaps wore off, a thought ran across my mind. *Maybe she was getting her turn to ruin my name at work like I had attempted to do to her all those years back when we fell out.* That time I thought she threw a cigarette butt into my new car. I told her job that she was on probation for possession and wearing an ankle monitor. I dared the lady I spoke with to check Darby's right leg for confirmation. I never knew what became of that phone call, if anything, but maybe the chaos she caused by contacting my broker with that extreme lie, was her way of letting me know.

My Ex, Wyatt, explained how he tried to contact me during my incarceration. His unanswered calls coupled with a panicked phone call from Tai sent them both on a wild goose chase. Tai's first call was to my parents, who were harder to penetrate for information than a POW from Russia. Then, about five days into my stay, I had a visitor. At first, I thought it was the public defender I requested. That was immediately followed by a sudden panic as I thought about the possibility it could be someone from my office coming to confront e. In jail, you don't know who your visitor is until you walk into the visitation room, and at that point, it is too late to hide. To my surprise, it was Wyatt.

I must have been a sight for sore eyes all decked out in my county blues and jail braids. I looked every bit of 17. Although we had broken up months earlier, his time and concern made me feel valued and comforted. During the allotted visit, it crossed my mind that he may have looked up my arrest record and saw Eric's name. If he did, he never brought it up. Years later he confessed to seeing me and Eric together but decided to keep quiet about it.

When my public defender finally visited, it left me with mixed emotions. He highlighted my chances of getting out due to my contribution to society, education, career, and family.

On the other hand, the recklessness and repeat offenses made it hard to determine the judges' stance on my freedom. He did mention that the arresting officer had been diagnosed with PTSD, Post-Traumatic Stress Disorder. He would use that to get the case dropped, but he made no promises. "It can go either way" is how our meeting ended.

The morning of my court appearance I was awakened in the wee hours to the sound of my name over the intercom along with those that had court appearance scheduled that day. We got dressed based on the court dress code. CCADC required us to put our sweatshirts under our county blue shirt so that the world could see the bold statement on our backs that read, "Property of CCADC." We were handcuffed, and chains were draped around our waists as we were escorted to the holding cell for breakfast.

Our slop for the day was runny oatmeal, burnt toast, and a meat-like substance placed on a cafeteria-style tray. Sitting in silence, waiting on the transport van to get us, I fought to stay positive, but I kept returning to the conversation with my attorney. *"It can go either way"*. In a place like that, hope is all you have when you have nothing else. I focused on the things that brought me pleasure or joy, like laughing with my girls, a great cup of coffee, watching a sunrise, a beautifully decorated home, or a family vacation on the beach. That helped keep my fear at bay.

When we arrived at the courthouse, we were placed in another holding cell, this time, we were separated, and my quiet thoughts were deafening. As each inmate was called to face the judge, silent prayers were whispered, and "good luck" was softly spoken. The hope was that the judge would be in a good mood and no one who came before you would piss her off. Before I was called, my attorney came to visit me for an update. He reiterated that it would be up to me to convince the judge to set me free. Unfortunately, there was nothing he could do. I felt the air leave my lungs and my body started to shake. What a letdown; I hoped he was coming to tell me that he had worked things out and all I had to do was appear, agree, and go home.

Given that I was already on probation for DUI, wiggling out of this through sympathy and prayers did not provide me any relief. I knew what I had to do… pray. Especially when he said I was facing up to three years for a second DUI in this county. I needed to convey my previous mistake and explain that I had been wrongfully accused by an overly aggressive officer that suffered from post-traumatic stress disorder. I only had moments to prepare before the lock popped open on my cell, and it was my turn to face my fate.

I cannot put into words how terrified I was. My heart was pounding so loudly that I could feel the vibration in my ears. I just closed my eyes and took a deep breath. I prayed for grace and guidance; That was all I could do. I heard the click of the jail door off in the distance and footsteps with intention; an officer appeared, and I was up to bat. To describe my physical appearance as pathetic would be a compliment. I was skinny, ashy, my hair was braided to the back, and my clothes were swallowing me up. As I entered the courtroom, I glanced in the seats and saw both my cousin Darby and Eric sitting in the back along with the arresting officer. My attorney came to meet me in front of the judge. Her silence while reviewing my file did not provide me any comfort, she failed to make eye contact and seemed annoyed.

When she finally spoke, she addressed me as Ms. Ellison and asked me the dumbest question, "Ms. Ellison, I see you were already on probation for DUI. You have a public defender, but I can't help but notice you have money to get your hair done."

I wanted to jump up on the stand and choke her out. But, instead, I thought, *Bitch, with all the stuff I'm dealing with, you have the audacity to comment on the braids I got done in jail in exchange for two packs of ramen noodles!* But instead, I respectfully replied, "Your Honor, with all due respect, my hair was braided in jail in exchange for two cups of noodles."

She asked why I resisted arrest and refused to take the breathalyzer test on the night in question, to which I replied, "Your Honor, I in no way resisted arrest; I just exercised my right to refuse to blow. I was pulled over for a blown headlight; I felt that should have been addressed at the very least." I felt my blood pressure rising, and I wanted to get real with this lady, but, as fate would have it, I no longer had control over my body. The words, how I spoke, and my demeanor were all being led by a higher power. I prayed for guidance before entering the courtroom, and it was happening. This was a fight I had to win, and if I had to tap dance for this lady, then that was exactly what I would do. I had to fight to keep her from revoking my probation. We went over my career, education, house expenses, kids, family and all this personal stuff for the entire courtroom to hear. Profanity almost escaped when she said the officer recanted his account of the incident and admitted his post-traumatic stress diagnosis after his second tour in Iraq. Wait! what?!

After that 25-minute interrogation, she knew she would let me go home. Not to mention that after the officer's revelation, I could have been released weeks ago. This is the type of shit that happens behind the scenes that make our criminal system, well ... criminal. Could I have sought some type of justice? Maybe. But like others before me, the relief I felt upon hearing that I would go home erased what could have been a valid counterclaim to the courts. This is how things remain the same. Even after basically stating that no crime had been committed by me, she deliberated in for an additional three minutes before saying that she would reinstate my probation and that the 45 days would count as time served. But not without a parting gift. 60 hours of community service for what? I had won and lost at the same time. This should have been thrown out and the arrest deleted from my records. Instead, I had to go back on probation with 60 additional hours to work for free while trying to rebound from 45-days of incarceration. Justice served ... emphasis on served.

About four hours later, I heard the words all jailed folks love to hear, "Bags and baggage," with my name preceding it. For all the bullshit she stirred up, Darby was waiting for me upon my release. With no access to a mirror, I could tell by her expression that my physical transformation was a sight to behold. Her first words were, "Umm ... we got to get you something to eat, but first, we going to see the bondsman." On the way to the bondsman's office, she decided it was a good time to run down all the drama she had encountered with Eric and their differences in the state of my affairs. These two were the foot soldiers for my freedom because everyone else resided outside of Georgia and had no power without residency. Eric had been released three days after he was locked up and was able to sign my bond. I needed to see the bondsman to sign off on my release paperwork and get his requirements to stay in his good graces. After we left the bond office, I needed to get my incredibly small ass into a bath and some appropriate clothing.

I was no longer behind bars, but I was far from free. The

system is designed to continuously remind you of what a fuck-up you are. The new challenge becomes getting things back on track despite the obstacles. This probably has a direct correlation to the high repeat offender stats. On a positive note, I had a few more days without the kids and a place to call home. The downside was my immediate "to-do" list, which consisted of 60 hours of community service, DUI school, fines/probation/reporting, finding a new brokerage, and getting my past due expenses caught up. I also needed to apologize to my parents and kids. I'm sure they were upset, afraid, concerned, and saddened by the news of my on again, off again affair with law enforcement.

With all the best plans laid, the reality of just how difficult it was to un-ring the bell of a bad accident with people who had over a month to draw their own conclusions had sunk in. I checked my voicemail and chose which calls I would return. I contemplated my storyline, took a deep breath, and started dialing. The second call was to one of the agents in the office. As soon as I started to speak, she interrupted me. "Hey girl, before you start, we know you were in jail. You can thank Rebecca for this; she was relentless about finding the truth of your whereabouts." I advised her to keep it amongst a small group of agents, but she insisted on letting John (my broker), and everyone else know. I sat there in silence and relief. Now that I knew what everyone else was thinking, I could react accordingly and address my absence with truth or silence. She explained that if it were her, she would just face the music and come clean. She was unsure how my broker, would proceed, but I should reach out to him and find out. I did just that, I contacted John to apologize for my absence and to get his take on my future with the office. I spoke very little and listened as John explained that the news of my personal life saddened him. He advised that, although I was a good agent, I should focus on getting my business in order. This rejection hurt me, but I respected his honesty and advice.

After five wonderful years of fun, friendships, and growth, my professional and personal lives collided. The victim was my career at my current brokerage. I took the walk of shame, collected my personal effects and a few last commission checks, and exited the building. My brokerage promised to give me a great reference if I needed it. They never asked me to leave, but I knew I could not stay. I interviewed with other brokers and found a new agency within a week. I had made some horrible decisions in life, and life had punished me in return. I was down at times but never out. I kept my head high, stayed current in my profession, and got my affairs in order. The devastation was not enough to take me out for long. I started to focus on new adventures and challenges with my new company. I had my first encounter with an awesome, emotionally balanced female boss there. Her name was Diane. She was tall and thick and had a pair of boobs that made most people blush. She was a professional, and she ran her business like a boss. Fair, honest, diligent, and available, without the mommy persona that female superiors in my past operated with. This was my new home. Keller Williams Realty was a seamless transition from Coldwell Banker. The training was just as big here; collaboration and broker assistance were normal, so, to be honest, Keller Williams offered many of the same things my old office offered. The faces were different, but the hustle was the same. Sell homes, help families, make a great living, and have a blast doing it. I had a second chance at something I loved. I had been out of the game for almost two months and longed for the hustle and bustle of it all. I loved everything about it. I was not rich—far from it—but every dollar I earned came from hard and honest work. I figured the best way to forget my past was to create a better future.

For the first time in a long time, I felt like I was treading above water. It was not just real estate that captivated me; it was doing things with integrity and operating from a place of trust and enthusiasm that made me happy. I held on for over two years until the crash provided us with significant job losses, too much inventory, and decreased qualified buyers. So, like many others, I had to make some life adjustments during the housing market crash of 2007–2009. With a referral from a part-time agent/leasing consultant that lived in my subdivision, I interviewed and was hired as a leasing consultant for Foster Property Management. As I soon found out, I would be managing more than property. A more fitting title would have been property, people, finance, law, education, mental health, disaster, excuse, family, daycare, pest control, break-in, self-esteem, death/suicide/murder, and media manager. I was hired as a leasing consultant fresh out of real estate sales. This was a demotion.

The first of many mistakes, was taking a job out of desperation. I held on hoping the market would bounce back sooner than it did and that I could return to real estate. Instead, I ended up depleting what little funds I saved, and worked longer hours for less money. There were red signs everywhere when I started, but since this was going to be a "temporary" solution, I stuck with it. But three months into the job, it became painfully obvious that I would not be able to care for my real estate clients in the manner they were accustomed to. I begrudgingly contacted my sellers to announce my retirement from real estate and connected them with other great agents. As a realtor, I was good at negotiating deals for others, but I had failed to do the same for myself. I was officially part of the rat race and had sold my time for pennies.

To make matters worse, the regional manager promised me a position that would o use my marketing and sales skills at an appropriate salary. The first of many red flags was that the original property I was hired to work at switched the day before I was scheduled to start. It was an equal distance from my home, so I thought nothing of it. But when I arrived on that first day, the difference was obvious. I had accepted a position at a renovated property with a jazzy staff and progressive manager; what I walked into on March 23, 2007, was a wonderfully situated property with beautiful landscape. But unfortunately, the perks stopped there; the property was old, the staff was disgruntled, and the manager seemed surprised that I was her new hire. The bait-and-switch was complete, and I was unhappy from the start.

I began applying and interviewing with other management

companies immediately. After three months, I was offered a position at a more suitable property with an appropriate salary. I put in my two-week notice and start making plans for my exit. The Friday before my new position started, I got a call from the human resource department withdrawing their employment offer. I had not passed the background check, leaving me in a pinch. I sat at my desk for a minute to brainstorm and develop a strategy. Finally, I composed myself, swallowed my pride, and went into my manager's office. I asked her if she would like for me to stay. She said, "Absolutely," before I could finish. She just needed to run it past the regional manager. Crisis diverted! Although I continued to apply and interview with other companies. When it was all said and done, I had six offers withdrawn, throughout my time at Foster. It was always the same. Interview, offer, background check, offer withdrawn. I was paying for my sins every day. I was in hell. Residents and some co-workers often asked why I continued to work at that property. I always gave some lame excuse about "just until my kid graduates" or "the flexibility to get other things done," but the real reason was I had no other place to go.

Throughout my nine-year career with this organization, I had one interview for the initial position I was promised when hired. The position was for a traveling marketing specialist. Unfortunately, I believe I was interviewed purely out of formality. The company's trainer that conducted the interview violated every section of Title VII of the Civil Rights Act of 1964. She spent most of the time figuring out who would watch my kids when I traveled, instead of reviewing the role and responsibilities of the position. My attempts to steer the conversation back to the position details fell on deaf ears as she kept referring to my childcare. This was a direct violation of my rights and had I known it at the time, I could have saved myself an additional seven years of bullshit by recording this inappropriate conversation.

Years later, I was accepted into a master's program I would attend two nights a week. This program would benefit the company after my graduation. It was an accelerated program that only lasted a year, and I would need some leniency in my work schedule to get there on time. I requested to come in early and not take lunch on those two days. I had no idea this would become news throughout our company's region. For almost nine years, I accommodated pregnancy leaves, no show, people walking off the job, and repeated "call-in" offenders; I worked extra hours, traveled to assist other properties, and witnessed flexibility extended to other colleagues. Somehow that request was being treated like I was still in my probationary period. I was told to choose the program or my job. I was floored. The practice of granting a flexible schedule had been taking place at that office for quite some time, two of my previous property managers included. Currently, one of the leasing agents was enjoying a flexible and accommodating schedule. To further drive my point, my former manager stepped down to an assistant manager role so she could leave work every day at 2:00 p.m. (we closed at 5:30 p.m.) for six months to complete the prerequisites needed to start her own nonprofit. Oh, yeah! I forgot to add she was leaving the company after she finished her prerequisites. She was not leaving early to benefit the company; she was leaving early to start her own.

After that "chose school or your job" reply from human resources, I politely reminded the owners of these "other accommodations". This whole situation was laughable at best. Not everyone at the company agreed or practiced this type of foolishness, but it existed in key positions like human resources. Eventually, I was given the two days off early and immediately put under a microscope. The fact that I had gone straight to the company's CEO after being told, "No," initially did not sit well with some people. But fuck those people; after nine years a slave, I had things to do. After all, that was supposed to be a "temporary" position to supplement my income. A hundred and thirteen months later, I was still dealing with office politics. Four months into my program, I was fired. Peace!

***

The acting bug bit my oldest daughter Jaimee at a young age. She never shied away from an audience and loves to perform. Singing, dancing, acting, you name it. She had a lot of encouragement from my parents. My dad wanted everyone to learn to play an instrument, so he got Jaimee piano lessons. My mom loves writing plays, so Jaimee was in every school and church play known to man. Therefore, it was no surprise when she secretly auditioned for and was accepted to a performing arts school. I learned about her application and acceptance after the fact. One early evening after school, she runs into the house out of breath, holding the acceptance letter she had gotten. She auditioned during a recruitment visit the program made to her middle school. I was happy she was so excited, but hesitant about the school at which the program was offered. At the time, we were residing in the top school district in our county. My continuing financial struggles were partially due to living in great school districts.

Walton, our school district, was more aligned with my plans for my girls. Although Pebblebrook's creative opportunities aligned with hers. Walton school district is a nationally recognized blue-ribbon school of excellence, and I wanted both of my girls to take advantage of the college prep curriculum offered there. Having Jaimee switch course right before high school took a little more convincing for me than an acceptance letter. Finally, we agreed that if Jaimee wanted to go to Pebblebrook Performing Arts, which was 45 minutes away from our home, she, not I, would have to do all the leg work to make it happen. And that she did. I saw drive and passion in my baby girl; I knew she was interested in acting, but she went the extra mile to get all the necessary information, meet deadlines, located the nearest bus stop, provided testimonies, etc.

Laila and I attended a chorus performance at Pebblebrook during the first week of school, and I was sold. Those kids were amazing. We sat in the audience, speechless. It cost $3 per person to see the show, but it was worth so much more. The road ahead of us would not be easy, but something told me it would be well worth it.

Fast forward to her junior year, I scheduled an appointment to meet with her academic counselor. Jaimee was on track to graduate with distinction, and I wanted nothing to interfere. She had a tough class load, and the extra hours of rehearsals for plays, games, and other programs made it hard to prioritize. Up to that point, Jaimee's resume was impressive—Governors Honor nominee two years in a row, involved in many clubs and organizations, respectable GPA, college prep and honor classes, an overall solid student. That all changed once she got a taste of popularity. Against my wishes, Jaimee tried out for the dance team and made it; she had to spend her entire summer practicing. My plans were for her to focus on her studies and enjoy clubs and organizations that did not require excessive time, especially during the weekdays. Unfortunately, the dance team required countless hours of practice and faraway performances.

At the time of her tryouts, Jaimee worked at a local grocery store. As she got busier with dance, she slacked off with her other responsibilities. She started calling into work, missing her shifts, and eventually was let go. Additionally, she did not study as much and became a little rebellious and sassy. The meeting I requested with her counselor was both out of responsibility and a way to build a team effort to get Jaimee over that adolescence hump. Enter Corbin.

Corbin was an academic counselor, beautiful smile, personable and single. I've seen Corbin on several occasions, but it wasn't until one Friday night football game that I *saw* him. I requested the meeting earlier in the week for the following Monday, so when we spoke at the game to confirm our appointment, I was excited for more reasons than academics. It seemed as if the attraction was mutual. The flirtation started as soon as the meeting did. He started making comments like, "You and your husband," to which I kindly replied, "Umm ... it's Ms. Ellison." His second attempt at flirting was when he told Jaimee that she and her sister (referring to me) had a solid plan between now and graduation, but we should keep him in the loop.

The meeting was productive but loaded with hidden agendas. I developed a game plan to communicate my attraction to Corbin without overstepping my boundaries and putting him in a compromising position. Upon my arrival to the office that following morning, I conspired with my co-workers to validate my suspicions, but in a classy way. I drafted an email to Corbin that contained more than a recap of our meeting. His reply was full of underlined hints as well. Still too subtle to move forward with my plan, I put together a basket of goodies for Corbin and dropped it at the front office one morning. I was so nervous and anxious to get his feedback. The anticipation was driving me insane.

Around noon that little red circle appeared over the envelope in my Yahoo! Account.; I had a new email. The subject was "Thank you," and the body read, "I am *grateful* for all the treats you sent." *"Grateful!" What the hell does grateful mean? Did I just give him a ride home or something?* I called my friend Katie to get her take on his response. You know a girl needs her girls in the dating scene.

Anyway, if it were up to Katie, the counselor, and I would never have become an item. Her interpretation of the word "grateful" was more than humorous. She said "grateful" was something people say to each other in church, not a word used to show interest. ... point taken.

Although now, Katie's advice was noted, it t didn't feel accurate. I responded to the "grateful" email to get clarity from the source, and a few correspondences later, we had set a date for coffee. At the following Friday night football game, the counselor pulled me aside to confirm the best location and day to meet. I was so giddy I wanted to dance. There I was, at my daughter's high school football game acting like a student. It was awesome.

The day came when we were to meet for coffee, and I couldn't have been more excited and nervous at the same time. When I arrived, he looked just as sexy as I remembered. We ordered our drinks and got acquainted. He had a son with the ugliest name I have ever heard, had been married before, and had an appetite for learning that made me feel a little unprepared in some areas. The education gap was an unnecessary issue for *me* throughout our relationship. I kept it hidden from him, but the inadequateness I felt around this subject would come out as anger, jealousy, and distance. I never disclosed how empty I felt for not completing my degree. But it ate at me like cancer and built walls instead of bridges in some of my relationships.

On the other hand, Corbin had a lot of wonderful qualities. The main thing was his relationship with Jaimee, followed by his financial stability and willingness to make things happen. He was clean and neat and took most of the dating decision off my plate. Additionally, he had a great sense of humor, loved to laugh, had a diverse palate, and was proud and informed about his African American heritage.

After coffee, he asked me on an official dinner date that night. Of course, I agreed, and we walked three doors down to a restaurant where we continued to get to know each other over dinner and drinks. I enjoyed our conversation and looked forward to seeing where it might lead. The beginning is always so great.

The next day he asked me out to salsa, not sure if he meant with chips or the dance, either way, I was available for both. He lived a distance from my house, and the proposed salsa club was another

40 minutes from him, plus we both had to get up at six in the morning. So naturally, I said, "Absolutely." Hell! I like a spontaneous man. I drove to his place, and we rode together. We had a great time dancing, snapping pics, taking shots, and reminiscing about the songs and artists being played. He drove us back to his place and insisted I stay over and not attempt the long drive that night. I hesitantly agreed, while he made no effort to hide his excitement. The next day, he flew to Chicago to attend an educational seminar for work, we agreed to meet when he returned, and that, we did.

Over the next 10 months, we discussed a life together, took vacations, attended weddings and graduations, and enjoyed each other's company. That was the upside. The downside was his ex-wife, whom I never met. I spent considerable time around their son and found it strange that she had not tried to meet me. The other downside or pain point was his over-the-top passion for his fraternity. The man graduated from college almost twenty years earlier and was still barking and hugging fellow frat brothers like he had a starring role in Spike Lee's *School Daze*.

At the beginning of our relationship (which was made exclusive about nine days after our coffee date), Eric popped back up after a year's hiatus following his release from that prison bid. I had a bad habit of allowing this man to become a permanent fixture in my life at his convenience. A new relationship, marriage, or distance would not keep him out of my life, his words exactly. I considered him a friend, but he saw our relationship as more. I was at fault for allowing his interruptions in my life, but old habits die hard. He asked me to get away with him for a weekend during a lunch date. At that point, I only "really liked" Corbin, so accepting a weekend trip to the beach with my ex was easy. I lied and told Corbin it was a girl's getaway, packed my things and headed to Destin with my Ex. Corbin could have hit me with, "I'm coming along," but I chose a weekend when he would have his son, so he wouldn't try to tag along. But I could tell he was suspicious about the proclaimed girls' weekend, but he had no concrete evidence to dispute my story.

Eric was aware of my relationship, so he gave me space to communicate with Corbin while we were together. The choice to have a romantic weekend with my ex while entering a new relationship would come back to bite me in the ass, though; after all, Eric was my past, and I was damning my future with the new man in my life, fooling around with the man I never saw a future with. I was a woman with no morals; not only was I being deceitful to Corbin, but I was also keeping our relationship a secret from Jaimee. Damn, I had more secrets than the Secret Service in its entirety.

My dishonesty was only one of the problems. I insisted Corbin and my relationship stayed private. I didn't want him to disclose it to his co-workers or anyone associated with the school. I did not want my daughters to know until things became serious. As I envisioned it, we would sit my girls down and discuss our relationship. Maybe, I would say something like, "Surprise! Meet your new dad; I believe you two know each other," or something to that effect. Of course, plans are made to change.

One evening, Corbin phones to say he had tickets to the Falcons game. He continued, "One of the parents gave me tickets, and we will meet them first to tailgate." I was a little hesitant because a parent meant a student, which meant someone at the school would know we had at least been on a date together. But I went along with it anyway. Sunday came; we were headed to the Georgia Dome. We partied late the night before, so neither of us felt like getting up early enough to tailgate. But we made it for kickoff; the couple that invited us was already seated. Throughout the game, we chatted and cheered, and before we left, the wife wanted to get a picture with all of us. Corbin sat closest to the couple, and he said "sure" before I could object.

As soon as the flash went off, I knew we were busted. As we walked out of the stadium, I told him, "You know she asked to take that picture because she can't wait to show it to her daughter or someone else to help her identify the woman (me) that came with you." Then, I elaborated, "People are always interested in other people's personal lives; believe me, this will be a conversation before lunch tomorrow." Although he did not see things that way, I knew she had an ulterior motive.

. The following week, I noticed Jaimee was a little distant. On our ride home one evening, I stopped for gas. Out of nowhere, she started this random conversation about her friend at school and, how her mom went to the Falcons game on Sunday, etc. She continued, "My friend said Corbin was there." She went on to say how the friend's parents commented on how pretty his date was. When my daughter's friend was shown the picture, she immediately identified me as Jaimee's mom.

Silence fell over the car. I finally broke the awkward silence with, "did you see the picture?"

She replied, "Yeah. Are you and Mr. Thomas dating?" I did not answer immediately and danced around the question until later. When I got out of the car to pump gas, I texted him about the revelation. I was a little taken by her bluntness, but I knew this day would come. Later that evening, after dinner, I called Jaimee to my room to discuss my reasoning for not disclosing the relationship. I ask for her understanding, approval, and forgiveness. She was also hell-bent on hearing it from the counselor as well. The next day, in school, she stopped by his office to confront him ... respectfully. At that point, the relationship had been solid for quite a while, so it was okay that the cat was out of the bag. My girls liked Corbin, and he was great with them. We spoke about marriage and a future together. I met his family, and he met mine. I loved that he was close to his mom and siblings (his father had passed). It was a good sign to have a man with all around healthy relationships. I looked forward to the time we shared. His values were front and center, and I appreciated his willingness to express himself truthfully.

However, as time passed, his questions about my faithfulness throughout the relationship started to eat at our peacefulness. Whenever there was a disagreement, that Destin trip came up. He would ask the same questions and become frustrated with my same answers. I lied about Destin, but I had been faithful in the relationship once we became exclusive. Maybe I should have come clean and asked for forgiveness, but I was taught it is not what you know, but what you can prove. I knew he could not validate his suspicion, so I stuck to my story. Our interaction became forced, and you could tell we both were waiting for the other to blatantly fuck up so we could call it quits.

I the shift became apparent while retrieving him from the airport after homecoming weekend in Virginia. His kiss was a peck, he was quiet and wanted to order food from the drive-thru, and he smelled weird. When we arrived back at his place, he became preoccupied and cold. I couldn't take it anymore, so I confronted him about his deposition. Based on history, my thoughts went to one thing…someone else. The thought that he may be planting seeds in the next relationship while ours went unattended was upsetting. The counselor was the first man to break up with me officially, and it rocked me to the core. Partially because he beat me to the punch and broke up with me before I broke up with him; the other part was it was done so cold.

A few weeks after he returned from his fraternity weekend, I made plans to see the movie *Precious* with some of my girlfriends. I phoned him on the way to the movies to see if he wanted to meet us afterward or if I should just come to his house. Side note, we had only spoken once that day, which was highly unusual, so my call was twofold, to see which of the above would take place and to feel him out. He did not reply right away and seemed irritated by my questions. He finally said that he had his son for the weekend, which threw me off because for as long as we had been together, his weekend schedule had remained the same. I held the phone and counted, trying not to lose my temper and push him further off the cliff. Finally, I replied, "Oh, I thought last weekend was your weekend?" I continued in the most pleasant voice I could conjure, "well I could just come over afterward." His lame attempt at an excuse got the best of me, "Corbin! What the fuck is going on?" to which he replied, "I don't want to do this anymore."

My response was, "Do what anymore?" But I knew what he meant before he got it all out. I was asking questions I already knew the answers to. While this conversation took place, my crazy girlfriend kept calling me on the other end because she was lost. How do you get lost in Atlanta when you are from Atlanta? And when did I become MapQuest? The next twenty minutes consisted of me pleading for my relationship on one end of the phone and giving directions to Eva on the other. At the end of the call, Eva was headed home, I was at the theater, and my relationship was over. Besides, who wanted someone who no longer wanted them, right?

I ended up staying for the movie. I sat next to a group of ladies who were enjoying their "girls' night out". In the saddest scene of the movie, it was hard to stop my tears from falling for more reason than what was on the screen; the girl I sat closest to kindly passed her box of tissues to me. I drove home in silence that night. I could not sleep a wink. That breakup triggered feelings of abandonment, and my sadness quickly deepened into depression. The next morning, I checked my phone to see if Corbin had been bluffing. Nope. No such luck today. Not one missed call, text, or Facebook post—nothing. I reached out to him several times in the upcoming weeks with no reply. Part of me was relieved that neither one of us had to lie to ourselves about our future together. But the loudest part of me was saying I was inadequate and not good enough to seal the deal.

Less than a month after our breakup, I was surfing the internet at work, I pulled up Facebook, and the picture hit me like Mike Tyson in the second round. When you look for shit…you tend to find it. There it was pics of him and his new babe at the aquarium. Well, there goes any possible reconciliation. I had to run to the bathroom to avoid my co-workers and residents seeing me cry. I called my friend Katie from the bathroom and wept. She said,

"Faye, who knows? Maybe he will come around and want the relationship. Maybe he just needed space. Give it some time." Even though I probably would not take him back, it calmed me enough to go back to work.

Later that night, I revisited his Facebook page and took a long, hard look at the pictures he was so proud to post. Upon further observation, I realized that we would never have been that happy together ... ever. The right choice had been made, and now I would have to overcome it and move on. Sometimes salvation comes in the form of rejection. In this case, it came quicker for him than for me. It would be the difficulty of this breakup that finally forced me to seek professional help. I was taking it hard, and I could not shake the loneliness no matter how much I tried.

"You can't solve a problem with the same mind that created it"

Albert Einstein

We get oil changes to maintain our vehicle's performance, work out to keep our bodies fit, eat to nourish the body, and read to stimulate the mind. However, the above activities could not address the emotional and mental anguish I was experiencing. The breakup with Corbin left me drained and depleted. I had not felt that way since my roller coaster relationship with Laila's dad. I couldn't do the things I needed to do or be the person I needed to be for those who counted on me. I had tools but did not know how to use them. I needed help. Sitting in my office one afternoon, I decided it was time to get that help. I was used to living in a crisis but was not accustomed to being so empty. I cried all the time; I did not want to hang out. I crawled out of bed in the morning and ran to get in it in the evening. For me, counseling was an opportunity to understand my story, or the one I was telling myself, and put things into perspective. In the meantime, I made it through the days by completing my to-do list for Jaimee's pending graduation. It came so fast, and the race to submit college applications was at full speed. I avoided her school's campus as much as possible to lessen the chances of bumping into Corbin. It's interesting how things change; I looked forward to sharing Jaimee's senior year with him a year earlier. Instead, I was avoiding the mere mention of his name.

The push to college was the best distraction ever. Jaimee was flying in and out of state for auditions and interviews. She had a starring role in *A Raisin in the Sun* and basically lived on campus for two months. I was a mother on a mission. While Corbin provided her with all the waivers she needed, she and I put together a binder that included her resume, application, recommendations, and a business card with her major and GPA. We wanted to stand out, get accepted, and get as much money as possible. It was fun. The process was a lot to keep up with, and a lot of waiting, but I enjoyed every minute of it. Plus, I started to feel like myself again with all the college talk and travel. Little did I know someone close to me would set me back to first base with one strategically placed phone call.

Jaimee had an audition in Ohio one weekend, and the school paid for her and a few others to fly up. It was a beautiful Saturday fall morning when I dropped her off at the airport, and I was feeling better than I had in months. When I got home, I made coffee, curled up in bed, and watched TV with nothing planned for the day. The ringing of my phone startled me. It was Tai checking in as we had done for years. I'm private, so my intimate relationships are only surface talk with my girlfriends. Tai knew that Corbin and I were no longer together and how hard it was for me, but I didn't share much more. The motive of her conversation took me by surprise. I started talking about how excited I was for Jaimee and the audition. I assumed this cadence would continue, but I was sadly mistaken. She never acknowledged the news about Jaimee or anything I said. Instead, she went straight for the jugular. "I called because I see your beau has moved on," almost taunting me. My body stiffened as if I had seen a ghost. She was speaking of the picture I saw a week earlier. The one that made me run into the bathroom to weep. That is why I called Katie and not Tai when I first saw the picture. I knew Katie wouldn't judge or blame me. But there I was, listening to someone who should have been protecting me rip me a new one. My heart was beating so loud that I could barely make out her words. B u t n o t t o w o r r y, when I didn't respond, she was more than delighted to repeat herself. "I saw a pic of him and his new woman on Facebook."

Maybe the tears I cried or the sadness in my voice over the last few weeks did not convey how broken and depressed I was about the breakup. But this was no way to feel me out. I just saw that post the week before, so being reminded and teased about it was devastating. I could no longer breathe and felt myself becoming light-headed. The anxiety attacks that I had in the past were starting all over again. Tai's perfectly timed torture was nothing short of betrayal. I ended our conversation quickly and turned the TV off. I allowed myself to drift off to sleep to clear my head. I called my therapist to schedule an emergency session for that upcoming Monday. This was not the first time "my friend", "my ace", "my sister" had shown this side of herself. I needed professional advice on handling my feelings and addressing Tai's behavior.

My therapist Natasha used to give me tasks and assignments to complete. Her purpose was to help me see my situation from a different perspective. In therapy, my opinions, feelings, and thoughts were free to roam the room while she helped me understand my interpretation of things and to empower me. I know there's a stigma attached to talking to strangers or "airing your dirty laundry" in some communities, but in an era where people share death, divorce, pregnancies, promotions, affairs, political views, and everything else on social media, sharing your problems with one more person should not be a problem. The ability to face my truth and see who I was in the world helped me manage stress, develop stronger relationships, and offer inner peace like no other remedy had (i.e., drinking and sleeping around). Unfortunately, after that shit Tai pulled, I needed third-party assistance fast. "Grateful' that I'd discover the healing powers of therapy, I couldn't wait for Monday's session.

My therapist suggested I write a letter to Tai; that way, if she got upset, she could go back as often as needed to understand what I was saying. She further suggested that confronting her on the phone would just start an argument, and neither of us would be heard. Writing would allow everyone to hear the other, either now or later. It sounded less aggressive, so I agreed. After leaving my therapist on Monday, I returned to my office, closed my office door, and wrote the following to Tai via her Facebook DM:

Hey Tai, I wanted to touch base with you about a few things that have been on my mind for quite some time. Your disposition about relationships, rather yours or others, can be a little off-putting. Calling me early Saturday morning just to tell me that Corbin had moved on was rude and inappropriate. You didn't even take the time to acknowledge the exciting information I told you about Jaimee. I can't imagine what would make my best friend say some of the insensitive things you do. For example, around Thanksgiving, you asked me, "Isn't it funny how a guy acts like he is in love with you, and when you break up, he's already sleeping with somebody the next day? Oh! I don't mean Corbin, but I'm just saying." Tai shit like this has been going on for years. When Galvin and Alexis were engaged, you said to me, "I always knew they liked each other, even back in school." (How fucked up was that for you to say?) Then the constant updates on Owen. I've seen you do this with other people's relationships as well. IT IS UNACCEPTABLE for you to be Facebook friends with my boyfriend (past or present). He does not want to be your friend. You have always been weird about being close with your friend's significant others. The comment about guys moving on sexually and Corbin with his new woman triggered a small panic attack. You have no idea what that relationship may have meant to me. I have given our relationship some thought, and the inappropriate things you've done sometimes have put a strain on me. I am not physically capable of receiving negative energy from anyone at this point in my life. I'm a work in progress, striving to become a healthier, happier, more spiritual person every day for my family and me. I can no longer allow anyone else's insecurities to become mine.

I value our friendship and sisterhood, but there need to be boundaries. Anyone I have dealt with intimately is off-limits for discussion. I need some time to reflect on this; maybe you should too. I'm not perfect, that's why I'm getting help...maybe you should too. This email may upset you, or it may enlighten you. Either way, I can only be a part of your life if you want a cheerleader, a positive support system, and a real friend. I am no longer available for anything else. I expect the same as it relates to your relationship with me. I still love and care about you, but this behavior must stop.

She replied: *Hey Faye, first of all, you are absolutely right, your message is rude and disrespectful, don't send me a negative letter through email, Facebook, or whatever, be woman enough to tell me to my face or at least by phone. I didn't become friends with Corbin on Facebook to talk to him, I was adding friends just like you were to build my friends, and if I brought up all your insecurities from our past, I'd still be talking. I'm glad you are seeking counseling, you probably do need it, and I know I'm not perfect, but I can accept it; I'm a work in progress also. You really need to look at yourself before you throw stones. I've dealt with your alcoholism and flaws as a mother, but I didn't try to ever badger you about it. I only always built you up. And by the way, I didn't befriend your ex-boyfriends; they befriended me! And you encouraged our friendships, so like I said, that's great you are seeking counseling, but don't come at me because you are no better than me. I love you and your children, and I always will but focus on getting your life in order like you said. May God continue to bless you and your family. Tai.* This conversation took place on February 22, 2010. Our relationship suffered for over three years because the conversation never went further than this DM communication.

I don't regret sending that email, and I appreciate her reply. It made me feel a sense of peace to finally say what needed to be said and be okay with the outcome. Addressing Tai's behavior over the years was part of my healing. I had to create boundaries and standards in my relationships. One at a time. Everyone has a story they tell themselves; I could debunk some of mine through honest communication. It took longer than I had hoped, but the process was in motion. After being betrayed by my guy, then my friend, I needed to take inventory of those closest to me. Everyone needed to be categorized; sharks (vicious and selfish) in one box, tunas (indecisive and victim mentality) in another, and, finally, dolphins (cheerleaders, protectors, supporters, mentors) in the "keep open" box. I got these titles from a book I was given by my broker called *The Wealthy Spirit* by Chellie Campbell. In the book, Chellie uses the analogy of fish in the sea to describe different character traits. I needed to fill my team with dolphins while learning to be a dolphin for those in my life. Not many people had gotten as close as Tai, but the lesson was learned. Time does not equal position. From then on, people would have to earn whatever position they were given in my life, as I had to earn mine. No hard work or complicated tests are required, just respect, thoughtfulness, and honesty.

LOST AND FOUND

Before the above took place, Tai and I talked all the time. She owned her own cleaning business, thus providing her with more flexibility to converse throughout the day. She often called my office to chat during my lunch breaks. If my manager answered the phone, she would hang up but would engage in conversation with my other coworkers if they answered. So, the one-time my manager came into my office and delivered a message from Tai; I knew something was wrong. I nervously asked, "Did she say anything else?"

She shook her head no. "Just that you should call her right away."

Something had to have happened for her to leave word with Pam.

I took a deep breath, grabbed my cell phone, and walked toward the restroom. Tai answered on the second ring; then she paused, cleared her throat, and said, "I called to let you know that Viv passed." The words jolted me, and I had to grab the counter to keep from falling. I heard the pain and sadness in Tai's voice as she continued.

"What! What happened!" were the words I managed to get out.

"She had a heart attack an hour ago." She must have heard my muffled cries and confusion. "I know; I'm in shock, too," Tai said.

Viv was on the phone with her oldest son when it happened.

Vivian "Viv" Johnson was the craziest, most loyal, and honest person to ever walk this earth. She didn't care who you were; if she had questions, she needed answers. She was short, adorable, and had been planning her wedding since middle school. She loved being in love, and we all loved her. Nobody in Atlanta knew about my sister Viv, so they could not understand the devastation I felt from losing someone I did not speak directly about. But if they knew her, they would have loved her too. Viv was my sister from another mister. The old crew—Tai, Cali, Viv, and me. Now her sudden death had created a different bond among those left. Her passing made us all consider our mortality. From kids on the playground to teenagers falling in love to parents raising kids and wives building a life with our partners, we never thought much about death. Viv had previously fought and won against breast cancer, but the treatments caused her congestive heart failure. My sister suffered through sickness, hair loss, loneliness, and the challenges of raising three sons, all while keeping her wit and sassiness in tack. When she beat cancer the first time, I took it for granted that she would always prevail. I never considered that anything could take her away from us, but on that day, I was proven wrong. There I was again, in the bathroom at work, weeping. I scheduled time off and booked a flight to attend her homegoing service.

Life can be messy like that, we were on the dance floor a year earlier at her sister-in-law's wedding, jamming to Beyoncé's "Get me bodied." Now I was packing for her funeral. If I had known, it was our last encounter. I would have emphasized how much she meant to me, and I would have kissed her chubby cheeks and held her until it was awkward. Damn, I cried for days. As I write this, I can feel the sting of tears surrounding my eyeballs. I cried because it was cruel; I cried because she had spent so much time winning against cancer only to lose; I cried because I didn't get a chance to say, "I love you, sis, and it has been pure joy kicking it with you all these years."

Her funeral was only the second time I saw Tai since our

Facebook exchange, which was weird as hell. The four musketeer pictures were displayed at Viv's funeral. As we affectionately called her, Viv, and Cali's mom, or "Mama," had pictures displayed in the church lobby. I looked at the photos that seemed to have been taken a lifetime ago. Me, Tai, Cali, and Viv as kids. Smiling for the camera without a care in the world. But here we were as adults, beefing with one another and burying the other. I sat on the family side of the church during the service but not next to Cali or Tai, which made my heart ache even more. I needed my sisters, and I knew they needed me. Timing.

After the funeral, I went to Tai's house for about an hour, full of surface conversation and nervous laughter. I ended the night with Cali and the rest of the family, where I shared and enjoyed stories about our time with our sister. Rest in peace and happiness, Vivian "Viv" Johnson; I will always love and miss your crazy ass.

"To raise a child who is comfortable enough to leave you means you've done your job." Author Unknown

Therapy had me dating beneath myself, beside myself, and everyplace else. I decided to end discussions on intimate relationships in therapy and focus on more important things. Who I slept with or who asked me to marry them became less important in my sessions. The year was 2010, and Jaimee was graduating from high school without one of her biggest cheerleaders in attendance ... my dad. Natasha worked to prepare me mentally for the possibility of running into Corbin during Jaimee's graduation ceremony. Jaimee was the senior class Vice President and was slated to give a speech, and he volunteered at every graduation. Secretly, I hoped to run into him so that he could see how great I looked while he looked as if he had added 20 pounds (via Facebook pics). The other part wanted to avoid the encounter to keep a healthy distance from the man who left me. Fuck him; he had moved on, and so had I.

With that possible crisis diverted, I had another crisis floating around the ceremony. Natasha and I never discussed the possibility of my dad not participating in Jaimee's graduation festivities, which was more concerning than running into my Ex. My dad had been there for my daughters since their births. But especially for Jaimee, since her dad was not in the picture, Paw picked up the slack. He did everything for her, and they were close. His absence was hurtful, leaving all in attendance saddened and confused. He and my mom had separated three years earlier. My mom moved out when my dad was at work. And he had not forgiven her. He was in his feelings and refused to be involved in an event or a conversation that included her, thereby punishing himself and the rest of us with his immature decision.

Despite his absence, Jaimee's graduation was a huge success, she nailed her speech, and the after party was a blast. My mom, Kei, and future sister-in-law flew in for the occasion, and Darby was in attendance with her new baby. The village had done it! One down and one to go. The sky was the limit for Jaimee, and that was all I needed. I had a permanent smile for more than a week afterward. That's what happiness felt like.

After getting Jaimee settled into campus life, I decided it was time for me to return to school and finish my degree. I was sitting at the office one afternoon and submitted a request for information from a university. Minutes later, I received a call from an enrollment specialist. Soon after, I selected classes, ordered transcripts, and applied for financial aid. This was one of the best personal decisions I'd made in quite a while. I always felt incomplete not finishing my degree, but the path to my redemption started that day. This thing hung over my head like my felony record. But the weight was lifted just through enrollment.

The embarrassment that once consumed me was replaced by enthusiasm. I was a woman in repair and man did it feel good. On that first day, I drove to school with pride. When I took my seat in the class, it was as if I had been elected to sit on a prestigious board. I balanced work, school, and parenting effortlessly. School made me feel like I had given myself a second chance to do it right. The "going nowhere" treadmill I walked daily on my job was easier now that I was doing something to change my situation. I was on an upward spiral and mentally separated myself from the environment I worked in daily. When I received a 100% in my first class, I was on cloud nine. I was going to eradicate mediocracy and finally live my best life. I discovered that I perform better with a full plate. Idle time was never a friend of mine.

MORE OF THE SAME

"WTF!" But before the words left my lips, I recognized the man-like bitch jumping out of the vehicle. She was yelling and pointing a gun in my direction. The truck with the flashing lights blocking me in was my welcome back to reality.

"Turn the vehicle off," yelled the lady.

I yelled back, "Who the fuck are you?" but I knew the answer. Two weeks earlier, I received a call from an employee at the PO Box location I had used for years. She started the conversation off by asking me if I was okay. I thought this was odd; we were cordial but not close enough for her to pick up the phone in the middle of the day to check on my well-being. I replied, "Hey! I'm good. What's up?" I was further confused when she replied that the GBI (Georgia Bureau of Investigations) had just left the store looking for me. Despondent and concerned at the same damn time, I asked some fact seeking questions to get my bearings. While this conversation was taking place, my dad was clicking in on the other end. I ended the call with the store attendant and clicked over to speak with him.

As soon as I answered, he said, "What kind of trouble are you in now, Fatou?"

I replied, "I have no idea; I haven't done anything illegal in quite some time."

My dad told me how the GBI called the house looking for me and said they were checking all my last known addresses. I filled him in on the call with my PO Box location, and he gave me a name and number to follow up with. "Okay, thanks; I'll call them now and keep you posted." I hung up with my dad and took a deep breath. Anyone observing this ordeal could have seen my heart beating through my shirt.

I dialed the number and asked for the name I was given; the rude bitch on the other end started by saying that she needed to know where I lived, and that I needed to turn myself in. I was like, "Whoa! Whoa! Whoa! Hold your horses, Missy. For starters, who are you? What is this about? And who is this about?" She explained in the most disrespectful tone she could muster that there was a warrant out for my arrest for food stamp fraud, to which I sort of giggled and said, "Did you just say food stamps? Ma'am! Let me understand you correctly. Are you telling me that you and someone else got into your official vehicles, drove to my address (which you saw was a UPS store) looking for me, and then drove back to your office and dug through files to find my parents' home address and number and then called out of state about some fucking food stamps? I'm just verifying that the person on the other end of this phone is indeed a food stamp cop…am I correct?" I probably should not have been such a smart-ass, but please. "You must be one whack-ass officer to be placed on food stamp cases. Then, to add insult to injury, your ass is calling and harassing people all over the nation about this shit with so much vigor in your voice that people think I have joined Al Qaeda or some shit like that. Nope, instead, they will find out their tax dollars (and mine) has been allocated to pay the salary of people to chase down motherfuckers buying ketchup and ground turkey."

This set her off, and she was like, "Miss Ellison, when are you coming down to see me? When are you turning yourself in?"

I said, "Let me take all this in, get an attorney, and I'll be down there as soon as possible." I disconnected the call and started investigating the potential fallout.

She was right; these people were serious about their government assistance. So here I sat in my vehicle on this faithful night after working all day and attending school all evening. Now it was the officer's turn to be a smart ass, and the food stamp case had come knocking at my front door. The aggressiveness of the undercover officers tickled me. Unmarked truck, man, and manlike woman in plain clothes; had it not been for the flashing light, it's fair to say they deserved to get fucked up. Story of my life: hard-working citizen and student by day, wanted criminal by night. My neighbors must have thought, "Wow, just when you thought you knew someone."

I was apprehended and placed in the unmarked truck. But the kicker, Laila, was in the house. Let me be clear: I was more concerned about her missing school the next day than anything else (including my job, my lease, etc.). I politely asked the officers if they could get my daughter so I could give her instructions on what to do and let her know what was happening. They coached Laila downstairs from our apartment (after she heard me calling her from the back of the truck). I was able to give her some instructions before I was hauled off to Cobb County Correctional facility ... again.

While in transit to jail, I had to think figure out how to keep things intact. After all, I had to be at work the next morning, and my child had to be dropped off at school, but all of that would have to take a back seat to the issue at hand for now. The time was approximately 11:00 p.m. when I was taken into custody, so I had the girls reach out to my old faithful, Eric, and my Darby to start raising money and making calls to bail me out. From there, I knew Darby would reach out to my parents. She was prohibited from contacting anyone besides them. There was no need for history to replay itself fully. My job, friends, and associates were off-limits (remember, this is the same cousin who had me in critical condition with my previous employer).

I stayed incarcerated for a little over 48 hours. While there, I had Jaimee call in the evenings, leaving a voice message (so I would not be fired for a no-show, no call after six years of service). I was finally released around midnight on the second day. Eric and Darby were in the parking lot waiting on me...again. They took my smelly ass home, as I rehearsed a proper performance for my employer and coworkers the following morning. When I got in the office, I met with my manager (whack-ass Jessie) and gave very little information to my nosy co-workers. By this time, a couple of employees from another property had started calling me to ensure I was okay while trying to collect intel. It did not matter who called or checked on me; I had experience sticking to the script about my time missing, no matter who asked. The consensus was that I had quit, so I rode with that scenario. I said, "I had a couple of days to rethink my decision." I suspected one person figured out what happened but had no proof.

I never saw that coming. Karma is a mother. Getting arrested for misrepresenting my income on a food stamp application never crossed my mind. It was wrong, and it was illegal. Little did I know that would be the case of all cases for me to rebuild from. The added stresses of restitution, reporting monthly, and the new record was almost enough to make me say, "fuck it." It became increasingly harder to get a new position, and the walls that were once widening, started closing in on me again. I felt more trapped than I had in jail. Having a couple of DUIs more than five years ago was one thing, but having a fresh felony was another pile of bricks. The only way out was to remove the bricks one at a time. That is what I planned on doing for as long as it took. I mustered up the energy to put a fake ass smile on my face, get through the days, and study during the nights.

The pressure to perform like nothing was wrong proved challenging but familiar. One side effect of faking it, I had become increasingly anxious, cynical, and angry. I no longer gave passes for bullshit, and the time it took me to go from zero to 60 shorten, and recovery took longer. My irritability level was at a two on a scale of 100, and I was snapping at people for the smallest things. I needed some peace and a good distraction from it all.

Who knew it would come at the most unexpected moment from the most unexpected person—an R&B singer from my favorite group?

IF IT ISN'T LOVE

Jaimee had flown to Atlanta for an event, and I was dropping her at the airport to go back to school. She over packed for her checked bag, so I had to hop out the car to help remove some things from her luggage. As Jaimee returned to the curbside check-in attendant, I exchanged glances with a familiar face. I looked at him and returned to what I was doing, but he kept staring. Finally, we exchanged glances again, and he smiled and waved. I thought to myself, *where do I know him from?* Before I could think another thought, it came to me. Wow! This was a member of one of my favorite R&B groups. I chuckled to myself as I joined Jaimee in line to finish her check-in. From a distance, I could hear someone saying, "Oh wait! I got it, she's right there. Here she comes." Those were the words of that R&B guy as he ran to my vehicle to ward off the officer approaching my unoccupied car. After a quick hug goodbye, Jaimee gave me a wide smile and head nod of approval as she disappeared through the airport doors.

Mr. R&B had gotten back in line to complete his check-in but not before asking me if we could exchange information after he took care of his bags. "Sure," I said and bought a little more time with the officer as I waited to get closer to someone, I'd been a huge fan of most of my life. He returned to my vehicle, and I gave him my business card and put his numbers in my phone. I truly didn't expect to hear from him. I went about the business of life, and one day, while at the office, I got a call from a number unfamiliar to me. I let it go to voicemail the first time but decided to answer it two days later when it called twice in a row. It was him! I thought to myself, *oh my God!* as I sat at my desk and conversed with a musical legend.

My attempts to keep things in perspective failed as he aggressively pursued me through calls, texts, and long conversations regularly. Although not the sexiest member of his famed group, he was the businessman amongst them all. My online search answered one of my suspicions, he was married. So, I thought the relationship should stay in the friend zone. But from the start, his comments, suggestions, and invitations let me know he thought otherwise. I wondered how he planned to do what he wanted with me without being exposed.

His group was slated to perform in New Orleans for the annual Essence festival. However, before the big performance, the group met in Atlanta to rehearse for two weeks. I saw him often during his time in Atlanta. I was a little star-struck, but his demeanor helped put me at ease. Over the upcoming two months, we would meet up, hang out, text, talk, and sleep together until it all came to an end when the group was scheduled to perform in Atlanta.

He made plans when he found out he would be in my town again. I went lingerie shopping the morning of the performance and packed my stuff for the concert. I borrowed my ex-boyfriend's Maserati and proceeded to my VIP evening in style. When I arrived, he was relaxing and, at his request, I joined him. He seemed distant, but I shrugged it off as pre-show jitters. He started asking me about marriage, dating in Atlanta, and my kids and their father. I thought the conversation was oddly timed, but I played along. Maybe he had done some online research of *his* own. He was aware that I knew he was married with three kids, but at that moment, I felt like I was the one cheating on *my* spouse. No need for the intimate details of our association, as he initiated everything that had happened up to that point, and I was just along for the ride with no expectations. It was getting closer to show time, and he reminded me he had reserve passes for Darby and me to attend the show. Then he apologized for his behavior yet continued repeating it. What the hell? Then he paused for a minute, kissed me, got up, and went to shower. Sensing our ride had come to an end, I went into the bathroom, said "Goodbye and good luck," and left. I didn't even grab the passes he left me on the nightstand.

Darby called as I was walking out, to let me know she was in the lobby. We still went to the show, enjoyed ourselves, and went home. The next morning, I had an early flight to Vegas, and my head was hurting from that enigma. I was hella confused about the events of the evening. I quickly thought, *we should have stayed in the friend zone.*

It would be a couple of weeks before I got the answers regarding his demeanor that afternoon. His wife was expecting. That was our last conversation. My biggest disappointment was that I didn't meet the entire group. Such is life.

"Now I know in part, but one day I will know in full."

1 Corinthians 13:12

BABY GIRL

It was Laila's sophomore year in high school, and she was preparing to spend spring break in Panama City, Florida, with one of her close friends and family. The year had been particularly tough for seasonal allergy sufferers, of which Laila was one. I wanted her to enjoy herself and not spend the entire week sneezing, blowing her nose, and putting ice on her eyes to minimize the swelling. In the past, Claritin Redi tabs did the trick, but this year saw no relief with the mild dosage. We spoke with a few people who also suffered from allergies and the pharmacist at our local store. We were constantly referred to Claritin D. I made the purchase, and Laila started on this seemingly harmless medication. She was on the medication about three days before the Panama City trip and was doing much better. We occasionally spoke throughout her trip, and things seemed normal. That all changed the day, she was due back in Atlanta.

She was frantic because she was scheduled to work the same night she returned. I was unsure why she was so nervous about being late when she could just call her manager to inform him or get someone to work her shift as she had done in the past. Furthermore, I did not understand why she scheduled herself to work on the day she was driving back from out of state, but I brushed it off. That afternoon, I dropped her at work on time and headed back home. About thirty minutes later, she called me, apologizing for earlier, she went on to say that she was not scheduled to work that night, but the following evening. My initial thought was maybe she was tired from a long week of fun in the sun. Turns out it was something more sinister.

I had this strange feeling in the pit of my stomach but chalked it up to weird adolescent behavior. But in the upcoming weeks, incidents like schedule mix-ups became more frequent. One of Laila's friends, Aimee, was having a "kick-back' at her home the following weekend after the Panama City trip. Aimee and Laila spent considerable time at each other's homes, and I was well-acquainted with Aimee's parents. Jaimee and I always had reservations about Aimee though; she was a little two-faced for our liking, but she came from a decent family. I hesitantly agreed to let Laila attend the kick-back, with strict rules to follow. The evening of the party, I did a quick walk-thru with Aimee's parents when I drop Laila off. The party was held in their fully finished basement, packed with entertainment, food, and teenagers. I left feeling good about my choice to allow her to attend. That was on Saturday.

The following Monday, Laila texted me and said she wanted to talk when I got home from work. When I got home, she talked to me about her childhood like we'd never met. I stood in the dining room for about 45 minutes waiting for her revelation, but the conversation seemed to go nowhere. I noted that she looked drunk or high and had this irritating smirk on her face the entire time. Her words were abundant, and she talked in circles, often losing track of her thoughts or changing stories. I was confused yet relieved that I would not be a grandmother or need to hand over a load of cash to bail her out of some nonsense she had gotten into. But, deep down, I was worried.

The days following this conversation would only get weirder. While at the office, I received a phone call from her school around 3:45 p.m., the school's nurse left a message for me. She asked that I not be alarmed but should call as soon as possible. I took a couple of deep breaths and returned the call. Mrs. James from the school stated that while in math class, Laila laid out on the floor and requested the presence of a classmate who did not attend that school. She was in a sedated-like state and laughed without being provoked. After several attempts from her teacher to assist her, she was instructed to go to the nurses' office, where she was later frisked and searched for drugs by the school's officer. I was also informed that she sat through her math class twice because she wasn't sure she was present the first time. My heart stopped throughout the conversation, and I was angry that Laila was either high or drunk at school. I picked her up and attempted to have a parent-child conversation, only to be further frustrated by her demeanor.

The next day, I dropped Laila off at school, and before I could make it back home, the school was calling me again. After this happened three days in a row, Laila was ordered to get an evaluation. She would not be allowed back on campus until she was cleared by a medical professional. Things just kept escalating. While I was in school one evening, Laila called me. I excused myself from class to answer her call. To my dismay, she asked me for our home address. At first, I believed she was joking, and I quickly reminded her that I was in class and taking finals. She called back 10 minutes later to ask me where *she* was. My laughter stopped, and the cursing began. "What the hell do you mean? Where are you? How am I supposed to know?" By this time, I was starting to get light-headed and fought off a blackout. "I thought you were at home."

She said she thought she had to work and ask one of her friends to take her there, and now she was walking back home, but couldn't remember how to get there. While my brain is attempting to process her words, she started to panic. She was afraid because a dog, who was on top of a vehicle in the parking lot was staring at her.

I looked at my phone, then behind me to see if someone was recording me being pranked. No such luck, it turned out this craziness was real. I instructed her to go back inside her job and wait for me to finish my test and drive to her job. I went back into class, hurried through the rest of my exam, and headed out to get her.

When I arrived at her job, she got in the car. Before I pulled off, I asked her where her purse was, and she smacked her forehead with her hand. "Oh! I know where it is!" she then walked back inside and pulled her purse to of the trash can. I phoned my mom on the way home because I was scared and needed to speak to a level-headed person.

When we got home, I sat in the car and instructed Laila to go into the house and start prepping for the next day. "Get your clothes out and get in the shower," were my exact words. Much to my disappointment, that is exactly what she did. When I finally went inside, I called out to Laila. My call went unanswered. I checked her room and then her bathroom and found her literally in the shower, sitting there, fully dressed. I immediately called and left a message on my office voicemail, letting them know I would not be in the following day. I spent the remainder of the night trying to clarify what was happening.

For the past couple of weeks, her literature class had read a book called *They poured fire on us from the sky*. She started blaming the book for her behavior, speaking about how it depressed her and how sad she felt for the children in the book. I thought my child was possessed, so I went a little crazy myself. I forbade her from finishing the book; I stripped her wall of all her posters and took away her phone. That night, I lay awake and prayed for an understanding. I prayed to God that he would show me the root of the problem because I was lost.

When I awoke the next morning, I could only remember a picture of the Claritin D box from my dreams. I ran to her bathroom and hid the box in my drawers. Afterward, I peeked into her room to see if there were any changes overnight. I called her name and knew we were still in cuckoo bird land by her loopy response. This type of weird behavior became the center of our lives over the next two weeks. I experienced everything from uncontrollable laughter followed by uncontrollable crying. Her paranoia was increasing, at one point she packed up her things because she was going to get her own place. Damn, we back in a crisis. The overwhelming sadness and pure terror I felt, was unbearable. She couldn't be left alone, out of fear of her hurting herself or being hurt. At 16 years of age, Laila had to accompany me everywhere I went. Work, salon, store, post office, everywhere. She was out of school for a week with an endless list of doctors' appointments. Every time we saw one specialist, they referred us to another one. I visited everyone I thought could shed some light on her condition—a psychologist, psychiatrist, neurologist, therapist, and our pediatrician… Jesus! My real fear was that our hard work would be lost to a mental condition or drug addiction. It was eventually realized that the pseudoephedrine in Claritin D had caused her psychosis.

As the days passed and the Claritin D cleared out of her system, she started to walk, talk, eat, and sleep like herself again. The neurologist was necessary to ensure no long-term brain or mobile skills damage occurred. Thank God, everything was still intact and functioning properly. The psychosis my daughter experienced in her quest for allergy relief almost tore us apart. What a relief! no matter how short-lived it would be. Unfortunately, we would later learn that this was more than an episode.

THE EMPTY NEST IS UNDERRATED

2013 started as one of the best years on record. I felt a sense of calm and hopefulness. The girls and I were enrolled in college, and I hoped my efforts to complete my degree after a 14-year hiatus would motivate my girls to finish theirs. The residue of shame and self-doubt was eroding as my youngest child was headed to college, and my graduation was just months away. Those things provided a healthy balance as we dealt with my dad's absence, once again, from Laila's graduation. For the second time in a row, he let his issues with my mom keep him from celebrating one of the biggest days in his grandchild's life. It was bad enough her dad was unable to attend. Still, not having her granddaddy there was again unacceptable, especially since he led us to believe he was coming as late as the day before the ceremony. But the show had to go on. Kei, his lady, and my mom flew to Atlanta to see Laila graduate from high school. We avoided addressing the "pink elephant in the room" for the girl's sake. But dad's absence made as big of an impact as his presence could have. My dad was as stubborn as constipation for no sane reason. Six years separated from mom, and he was still with that bullshit.

Accepting my father's childlike behavior sent the wrong message to all involved. To his granddaughters, this signified the approval of selfishness, putting one's own needs above the greater good. For us, it validated the harsh reality of marriage and how no matter the substance built over the years, all could be reduced to a single act of defiance.

Regardless of attendance, as with Jaimee's graduation, we managed to focus on the day and celebrate Laila's accomplishment. We were two for two. There were no grandbabies; both graduated on time and went straight to college. The time had come to shop, pack, drive, clean, unpack and decorate for Laila's summer semester. Having to do it alone made me realize how dependent we were on my dad. I was surprised that he did not show up and go through the rituals for Laila's big send-off as he did for Jaimee. I could sense that it bothered and confused her as well. But I asked her to stay positive and know that her paw loved her dearly.

"Maybe something is going on we don't know about?" I said.

"Yeah, you know, paw," was her reply.

When my dad does not want to talk about something, he hides. He will not answer the phone or return messages. That is how he was with Jaimee's graduation and now Laila's. He also displayed this behavior when he was sick or whenever too many people were pulling at him for something. It was not the best way to handle things, but we grew accustomed to it. But he was our rock, and it threw us off when he shut down.

After I got Laila settled in, I called and left him a nasty message. I requested him to show Laila some support or call her on the first night at school. Instead, he reached out to Laila and promised to visit her and tour the campus. This was in June 2013.

THE MAN

I never saw my dad with more than a common cold. He wanted nothing to do with hospitals or doctors. At some point in his life, he decided that everything could be treated with 666 cold medicines, which worked for the most part. Unfortunately, it seems as if many men from my dad's generation avoided going to the doctor for one reason or another.

The rest of us had regular dental, vision, and health screenings, but not my dad. He took me to the hospital for both of my daughter's deliveries, and he was gone as soon as I was in the wheelchair. "Okay, call me when you're ready to come home," was his reply. After that, he was not coming in or hanging around a hospital longer than he had to. What a character, my wonderful, brilliant, stubborn, hilarious dad.

Adam Jackson Ellison served as a sergeant in the Vietnam War. Part of his detail required him to work on or around helicopters. These helicopters sometimes carried weed and plant killers. This was an important task for the US army because, in Vietnam, there was an abundance of bush, trees, and vegetation that made for great hiding places for the enemy. Agent Orange —or Herbicide Orange —was one of the herbicides and defoliants used by the U.S. military as part of its herbicidal warfare program, Operation Ranch Hand, during the Vietnam War from 1961 to 1971. Most foot soldiers like my dad came in constant contact with this herbicide. Years later, it would be discovered that it did more than clear out foliage. In the long-term, it would clear out health, ambition, and eventually … lives. A class action lawsuit ensued, and Vietnam veterans were encouraged to sign on to the lawsuit for financial reparations. My dad, who accepted no hand-outs and worked for everything he had, was not interested in being compensated, put on disability, or receiving assistance from anyone. The lawsuit went ahead without Adams's participation. My dad, like many other Vets, suffered from PTSD. At the time we didn't have the name PTSD but knew that trauma was a likely residue of battle. For as long as I could remember, my dad talked in his sleep and/or screamed to the point of waking himself up. The length of each episode varied but never failed to get our attention. We never knew how to respond, if at all, so we never did. Again, certain topics had no place within the home at that time.

Circling back to 2013, my brother Kei and I were conversing about Dad's attendance at one of our cousins, birthday parties. The word was, that daddy was the last person to leave the dance floor. The image of my dad letting loose and enjoying himself put a smile on our faces. As I listened to Kei describing that party, I envisioned my dad with his slanted smile and deep dimples, shaking his head to the music. "Kei, we should throw a party for Daddy!" I said with enthusiasm. He agreed, and we started planning for what would be "Sonny's Appreciation party."

Neither mom nor dad had celebrated anything big or small in a deserving fashion for themselves … ever. So, Kei and I worked diligently over the next several months from our home base in Atlanta and Houston to plan the event. We went back and forth several times about the type of party, colors, food, drinks, RSVPs, location, dates, etc. Throughout the planning, some of the same issues kept arising— money, schedules and getting an accurate headcount. We wanted to convey one message…We appreciate and love you for all you have been, all you are, and all you will be. It was a small way to pay homage to him for being such a wonderful, strong, and dependable rock in ALL our lives.

Birthdays are a given, whether you celebrate them or not, so we wanted to emphasize that this was an appreciation, not a born day celebration. My brother initially thought it would make more sense to have a birthday party for Dad in September, but I kept reminding him that we wanted to stick to the message and not mix the two.

As we worked to bring this party to fruition, we faced more than our share of challenges. One was the dates we chose that was the same day as our high school alumni annual picnic; the other was Laila's final exams and Jaimee's theater tour dates. Further fueling Kei suggestion to have it in September, as he so often brought up.

Before I could even respond, a voice out of nowhere said, clear as day, "You *don't* have that much time." It was not just the voice that shook me but the eerie feeling afterward.

I vehemently replied, "No! We can't change it," and from that point on the date was settled, No changing, no adjustments. The party would go on with or without whomever. After all, it was about dad, not everyone else. He was the last person on Earth for whom we should let anything, or anyone make us doubt our ability to pull it off.

July 2013 rolled around quicker than previous years, and it was time to execute. We finalized the location, food, DJ, decorations, tables, walk-thru, cake, drinks, photo booth, and red carpet. We even devised a clever plan to get my dad dressed up and in the building without him becoming suspicious. We told him we were taking family photos and that he and Mom would not be at the studio simultaneously. To stay true to our story, Jaimee and I stayed at my mom's place when we got into town the day before the party.

Notice I only mentioned Jaimee and not Laila because one of Laila's teachers would not allow her to take her final exam early. His exact words were, "If she is not in attendance to take the final on Friday, she will be given an F for the semester." "Really!" I was pissed, how could a surprise party be a surprise without one of his girls? I couldn't believe it, after we'd overcome so much to pull this off, Laila would not be in attendance. I never saw that coming. To make matters worse, it was the end of the semester, so I still had to drive to her school, pack up her stuff, drive back to Atlanta, and arrange for her to get home after her finals. Then I had to pack and drive to St. Louis, all within 24 hours. So, on behalf of Laila, my dad, my family, and myself, FUCK YOU, Professor Richardson.

The look on my dad's face when we surprised him was priceless. To see his friends and family gathered to honor him was worth every moment spent planning. The drinks were poured, the cigars were lit, the cake was cut, and history was made for us anyway. After four hours of non-stop dancing, drinking, eating, posing, and laughing, July 27, 2013, was in the books. Unfortunately, my mom did not attend, but with her help, the party came and went without any hiccups. Thanks, Mom. Afterward, some people stopped by the house to hang out with my dad, and the rest of us went to an after-hours spot frequented by our high school alums. It was a perfect ending to a perfect event.

The next day, my dad called to see if Jaimee wanted to see a play with him that Sunday; she said yes but passed out from exhaustion. I said I would try to bring her over there, but I had so much work to get in by midnight we never made it. By the time I was done, the show had already started, and Jaimee was still asleep. The following morning, we stopped by for a couple of hours before we hit the road back to Atlanta. As was customary, we always departed with, "I love you, and I'll see you soon." Little did we know just how soon it would be.

September 11, 2013, started on a good note. My beau called that morning to wish me a great day and confirm plans for later; the sun was shining; I had already got my workout in, and I was feeling great. I sat down to unwind before getting ready for work with a cup of coffee. A tribute to those lost in the events of 9/11 was on every station as I whispered a quick prayer for peace for those affected directly. I felt the tears fill my eyes as I imagined the victims, their loved ones, and the hate or conspiracy that caused it all. At that moment, I felt rich beyond money. I had my health, my family, friends, a job, a car, a place to call my own, and a plan. Tragedy has a way of putting things in perspective. People came together when the towers were struck in the name of justice. We were one. No color, no sex, no religion, no class, no position. So today was as good a day as any other to adjust and forget about any foolishness I allowed to persist in my world. I went to work with my head held a little higher that day.

Throughout my workday, I spoke with my brothers and mom. My dad had been fighting what he thought was cold for weeks. As his condition persist and worsen, he started avoiding my calls. Kame told me dad had not gotten off the couch much in the last two weeks and was not eating. Frustrated at dad, because since his first sniffle, I encouraged him to go to the doctor., I even attempted to get his insurance information to schedule a doctor's appointment, Dad had a rebuttal for it all. He didn't like doctors and hated hospitals and clinics even more. Eight days earlier, he called me to tell me that his cold had gotten worse. I told him, "Look, Dad, you have been paying into an insurance policy since 1978; I think you will be okay financially if you use it." I added, "That's what it's for!" As always, he agreed he would go but never did. I stalked him via phone until he eventually stopped answering my calls; and when he did, I would have the girls, and Kei, keep calling and my local cousins stop by to check on him. I took for granted he would get better. Neither my mom nor my brother could convince him to go to the hospital, so on September 11th, Kame called for backup.

A few of my dad's cousins went by the house and took him to the emergency room. I felt much better knowing he would get the medical help he needed. I asked to be kept in the loop and went back to work. Two hours later, my mom called. On the first call, she said my dad had spots on his chest, lungs, and brain. "Spots?" The doctors were running further tests to provide us with more conclusive information. I kept thinking, *Spots?* when I hung up, I sat in silence in my office. I turned off my computer, and the lights and stared at the wall. *Spots?* I jumped on the office golf cart to ride the property and clear my head. My staff was gone to lunch, and I was the only person in the office, so I locked up. I keep thinking, *Spots?*

When I returned to the office, my cell phone was ringing. This time it was Kei. Calm, cool, and collected, he wanted to know if I had spoken to Mom. I recounted our conversation, and he confirmed my worst thoughts. The spots were cancer, stage-four lung cancer, to be exact. They would keep my dad indefinitely as they performed more tests and developed a treatment plan, if necessary. I didn't give a damn about anything at that moment as I felt my insides start to stiffen. *Cancer!* I ran to lock the office door as I was in no mood to entertain bullshit toilet or lost mail maintenance request from my residents. When my manager (a good friend) returned to the office, I broke the news to her. I told her I had to leave to be with my daddy. She agreed, I contacted human resources to start the process of a family medical leave of absence or FMLA and that was that.

September 11, 2013, ended as the darkest day of my life…thus far. My dad was diagnosed with stage-four lung cancer, and I did not have anyone locally to turn to. After work, I stayed at a friends. house for a little while to avoid being alone. It was times like this that I needed Tai to lean on. Unfortunately, my relationship with her was still weird from the Facebook exchange. On the way home that night, I sent her and Cali a text and asked them to pray for my dad. I told them he had been admitted to the hospital for testing. As soon as I hit the send button, Tai called. She started by saying she knew we had not been as close lately, but she was always available. Her kind words broke me down, and I pulled over and wept on the side of the road. Tai cried with me and stayed on the phone for a long time that night. I fell asleep sometime after 2:00 a.m. It would be my last good night's sleep for a while.

The next morning, I filled my cousin Darby in on the prior day's events; without hesitation, she booked me a flight for Monday. It was booked for Monday because I was throwing my friend a baby shower the following day. I wanted to honor my commitment (there was still so much to do) to execute the baby shower. I did not tell Eva about my dad because I wanted her to enjoy her day. I waited to tell my daughters, so I could provide more answers. Plus, I could not help them through this difficult time. I needed a little more time to accept what was going on. Not accept as in giving up but accept as in not being in denial and doing nothing.

I flew out on the morning of September 17th, and Tai and my niece picked me up from the airport. Kei arrived later that afternoon. When we got to the hospital, I was greeted by my mom. We embraced, and she brought us up to speed. My dad had been moved to the ICU after he collapsed in the restroom. It was discovered that he had a bleeding ulcer, and emergency surgery was performed; he lost an abundance of blood, and it was presumed that a transfusion would be needed. I wept as I imagined the pain my dad was enduring. His worst fears had come to fruition, and he was officially a resident of a medical facility. After surgery, he was placed on a strict diet and was under constant observation until he was stabilized.

Thank God for laughter, though, because even in his sickness, my dad was hilarious. He was not trying to be funny, but his constant attempts to escape his confinements were pure entertainment. He kept trying to remove his leg warmers and placed food orders with everyone who came into his room, and his attempts to bully Kame into picking him up kept me from getting any rest. I replaced my dedicated mother by dad's bedside. She had been in that uncomfortable room since he was admitted six days earlier. She packed her bags and moved into the hospital the day my cousins forced him to the emergency room. My mother, a real ride-or-die chick, "Till death do us part." After all the unnecessary bullshit he put her through, the anger, the control, zero communication after she left, no reply to letters she had written, my mom was, sacrificing her own comfort to ensure my dad always had a loved one at his side. If my dad had doubts about the love and loyalty of the woman, he had called his wife for 39 years, he could rest assured he made the best choice in a life partner.

My first night at the hospital was not a good one. My dad coughed all night long, something about the medication he was taking was causing acid reflux, and the jerk reaction from the hiccups continued to wake him throughout his slumber. He was a trooper, but I could tell he was annoyed and worried. Finally, he struck up a conversation about Jaimee's insurance policy and his retirement fund. Always looking to make someone laugh or lighten the mood, I said, "You know, if you die, I am not paying the $3600 I owe you, right?"

He shook his head and said, "I guess not, Fatou."

Two days after we arrived in town, my dad was well enough to leave intensive care and assigned a private room. The first order of business was to get him some food. The family sat in his room, ate fried food, and watched the Saint Louis Cardinals on TV. The next day, the oncologist visited us to review my dad's full assessment and treatment plan. There was NO good news at all. The cancer was aggressive, and the mass on his chest and brain was growing. The oncologist suggested my dad be sent for daily radiation and gave him three months to live. I was floored. The words poured out of his mouth as if he told my dad to work out and eat more vegetables. "Based on your test and our team assessment, I expect you to live for three more months at best." I videotaped most of the doctor's conversations so I could relate them properly to family members who were not present. I also recorded them for my research. Being in this predicament for the first time, my dad looked at my mom and me for a brief sign that we were okay with the proposed treatment plan. The odds were shitty, but so was doing nothing. I asked the oncologist, "If this was your dad or son, would you leave him here or take him someplace that specialized in this advanced stage of cancer?"

"Yes! I would definitely keep my father here; I believe our staff is one of the best," was his reply. He assured us my dad was in the best hands and trusted his own health to the staff.

My first call was to my brothers to see if we should just check our dad out and proceed to the nearest lake to enjoy his last days in nature. It sounded better than the artificial light and the sound of hospital machines. We could do a lot in three months, right? So, we started making calls to arrange for our dad to come home and live out his final days in his castle. We looked for an in-house nurse a medical bed and created a mock schedule so he could always have one or more of us around. Then reality hit, and the truth was the confusion and lethargy caused by his hypercalcemia. The hypercalcemia was why my dad lay on the couch at home for almost two weeks before being forced to the emergency room. Hypercalcemia is extra calcium in the blood and affects the entire body negatively. Stuck between what we wanted and what our dad needed to live for three months or more, we hesitantly agreed to undergo radiation.

My dad was scheduled for a series of brain radiation treatments to commence the following day. He was to be transported to a rehabilitation center daily and returned to the hospital afterward. This was a horrific decision, and his health's downward spiral accelerated. I started to read everything I could about alternative treatment plans and the medicine he was taking. Within a few days, I communicated with the doctors like one of their peers. I read enough to know what palliative care was as opposed to curative care. In my opinion, the doctors had given up. Not confident in the treatment plan, I contacted The Cancer Centers of America and got everything set up to get dad transferred and possibly another treatment plan. Everything was set; the hospital just needed a copy of his medical paperwork faxed over from his current facility. The problem was that only Kei, Kame, or Jaimee could sign off and release them. My dad was a strategic man. I did not always understand his methods or way of thinking, but he did.

He assigned Kei and Jaimee as his beneficiaries and Kei, and Jaimee and Kame over his medical care (healthcare directive). He seemed like a man who wanted to live, but his choice of medical care directives may have meant something different.

I told my family what I thought we should do and why. I was pitching my plan to a quiet audience on the other end of the phone. All it took was one of their signatures, and we could get the transfer complete. Since Kei was back in Houston and Jaimee in Atlanta (for the moment), I had to convince Kame to do it. After all, he lived in St. Louis and was the only one capable of physically signing the papers so we could get Dad into a cancer center for additional observation. For three days, Kame avoided signing the release before he finally told me he was uncomfortable doing so. I was completely outdone. His excuse was that dad would not want to be treated like a lab rat and have experimental procedures performed on him. I responded that we would have to agree to any procedure the doctors suggested; we would still have a say in his health and maybe with less invasive options. I just wanted him moved to a facility specializing in severe cases like his to evaluate him. I further pleaded my case, "if the center's recommendations are the same, we would know that we did all we could". Let's exercise our right to a second option; no harm done. Albeit there was a chance they would provide alternative remedies similar patients had found successful in healing or easing their pain. I might as well have been talking to myself. I had no consensus.

To date, I am convinced we should have done more. I was upset and disappointed to the point of numbness with my loved ones. It is human nature to survive, fight, and look for other answers. We had done more research for fucking car insurance than we did to help my dad fight cancer. It was my mistake to think we would display a similar hustle regarding the single most important figure in our lives. I was in hell. It was like standing in a room full of people screaming, "Fire," and everyone deciding it was easier to burn than locating the nearest exit.

Since being in that facility, my dad had received emergency surgery for a bleeding ulcer kept going in and out of consciousness. and shipped off to a rehabilitation center. A shit hole, by the way. From the minute we walked in, we saw unattended patients in wheelchairs. A nurse was talking and laughing on her cell phone, the rooms were dark and dreary, and there was a lingering God-awful smell of oxygen tanks or whatever the fuck sickening scent filled the thick air. To make matters worse, my dad was misplaced the next day after his radiation treatment. He was transported to the hospital for treatment and then left sitting in the cold outside because the driver had him listed as returning to the hospital instead of rehab. It was pure luck that my mom pulled up to the hospital when she did and saw my dad asleep on the curb in his wheelchair with nothing on his head (after his brain treatment). Tears ran down my face as I thought of my helpless father being left on the curb like he was some broke-ass beggar; I became enraged. This man had paid into his healthcare policy since June 28, 1978, and never used it except now, and the people responsible for his well-being had lost him.

I thought about the declaration the oncologist made *"Yes! I would definitely have my father here; our staff is one of the best."* Fuck that. I got on the phone to find out who was responsible for this mishap and to put measures in place to prevent it from happening again. To calm down from the stress, I went to the store to get cleaning supplies and candles to make my dad's room feel less like a facility. I stayed there into the wee hours of the night cleaning, watching Dad, talking to him even though he was asleep, and just taking it all in.

Because of the aggressive treatment, it did not take long for my dad's condition to worsen. We watched hopelessly as he pushed food away and became withdrawn and lackadaisical. It was my understanding that patients on radiation don't eat because everything tastes like metal. The food my dad craved just a few days ago now repulsed him. I kept thinking *His body needs nutrients and water to replenish and rejuvenate itself. Otherwise, how can he fight?* Then, two days later, my mom shared that he had eaten a small piece muffin, and to me, that meant he was on the road to recovery. Hallelujah!

My return flight to Atlanta was scheduled for Sunday, September 22nd. My college graduation was approaching, and I needed to pick up the girls. I spent that morning in Dad's room talking to him. Before I left, I had to get some things off my chest. I told him how proud I was to have him as a father. He was a great man, which was not a compliment given so easily these days. He had done much with what God had given him, and regardless of the outcome, he had built a legacy that everyone who knew him was better off because of. "You can lay there without frustration or guilt, and I can't wait for your testimony on beating cancer. I hate that you have it, but even with that, you are truly a rich man. You are also one of the smartest men I know, for you selected a great woman who remains by your side. I will see you when I get back with the girls. I am off to go graduate. I love you so very much." Before exiting the room, I wrote in bold letters on the nurses' whiteboard, "BEAT CANCER'S ASS, DAD!" Then I kissed him on the cheek and left for the airport.

I had several things to do before my graduation the following Sunday. I had to pick Laila up from school, continue my cancer cure research, and continue trying to sway my family into letting my dad transfer. That was a trying time for me; I waited almost twenty years to walk across that stage with my degree, I had waited too long to complete what I started, and I was going to walk across that stage, without my parents' or siblings' presence. But on a beautiful autumn day, Sunday, September 29, 2013, I woke up to a new iPad, breakfast, and a makeup artist to complete my look. All gifts from my daughters. I spoke to my mom that morning. Her calm words were like fresh air, "Enjoy your day, your dad will be just fine. We are not there in the flesh, but we are there in spirit." It was Jaimee, Laila, Darby, her husband, and the kids; two of my residents and Eric came to see me walk. It was bittersweet, but for that one beautiful day, it seemed as if everything would be alright.

The girls and I were due to hit the road back to St. Louis on Tuesday. With my dad's health deteriorating rapidly, the hospital staff scheduled a family call with the doctors, nurses, and our immediate family (mom, Kei, Kame, and my sister Joseline). Monday, September 30th, the day after graduation, I sat on the curb at Firestone while getting new tires put on my car to take the eight-hour drive to St. Louis the next day.

The doctors were adamant that there was nothing else they could do. This is where I could have inserted, "See! We could have taken him to Siteman's, and maybe we would be having a different conversation," but I erred on the side of caution and kept quiet. The doctors reported that my dad's organs were failing him and strongly suggested NOT resuscitating him if he went into cardiac arrest. They reasoned that his bones were too fragile, and resuscitation could do further damage as his chest may cave in, and on and on they went.

I asked them what his file said about resuscitation, to which they paused and then quietly replied, "Resuscitate."

I said, "With all due respect, follow the patient's request,".

During this part of our family call, I remembered a conversation I had with Darby about her mom's passing. She said that her mom told her she "was exhausted," and through her choice of words and actions, my cousin understood that her mom deserved peace from pain after several (years) of battling the rare liver cancer. Our situation was different. It was sudden, and we never got a second doctor's treatment plan. How did it come to this? Just two months earlier, we were drinking patron shots and wishing the rest of his life to be the best of his life. Fast forward to that day we were surrounded by strangers, telling us it was over, and we needed to get to St. Louis ASAP to say our goodbyes. Furthermore, it was just 19 days since he stepped foot in the hospital for the first time in my lifetime, and everything was moving too fast to grasp. I heard the words coming out of everyone's mouths, but I was not ready to throw in the towel.

After the call, I got my car and went home. I was to upset and discombobulated to drive that day, so we hit the road the next afternoon. I was intentionally taking my time and prolonging our departure. I put a game plan in place with Jaimee to have her sign for his transfer, and we were off to save Paw! We pulled off the exit in St. Louis near the hospital at approximately 11:23 p.m. that night. I called Kei, and he told me to meet them at the hospital. My mom and Kame met us at the entrance when we got there, and we followed them to dad's room. Upon entering, I noticed the eerie silence as Kei put on Bob Marley's "Three Little Birds," and my dad's heart monitor started to dance. I saw my dad was much smaller than the week before. He was frail, and his eyes were partially open. Without hesitation, both Laila and Jaimee crawled into bed with him. Even over the music, it hit me; the eerie silence was the absence of the machines he was once hooked up to. I was troubled and started reaching for the machine to plug it in. As I shared my finding with the family, my mom took a deep breath and whispered, "Your dad is passing to the other side as we speak."

Still in denial, I freaked out and started cursing and crying. There was no way this was happening. My mom followed me as I rushed out of the room to get some air. Minutes later, Kei was speed walking down the hall after us. "Hurry up it's happening!" We sprinted back to his room just in time to witness my dad take his last breath. Kei, Kame, Jaimee, Laila, our cousin Rohn and my mom. I watched my dad and tried to see if I could feel how he felt in those last moments when death crept up from his limbs to his torso. Looking back, death arrived at the hospital before we did. His hands and feet went first ... cold as ice from the soul abandoning them. But despite our efforts, death settled in his mind, and he could no longer stay. You could see the stiffness set in, and his body shut down organ by organ until he surrendered and took his last breath. Frozen. We just stood in silence as the head of the Ellison tribe left life as we knew it. I do not know why it came to mind then, but it did. Because of Laila's dumb-ass teacher, she didn't get a chance to dance with my dad before his departure. His party would have been her last chance.

But dad held on and waited for his granddaughter to arrive before he let go.

At approximately 12:02 am on October 2, 2013, my father was pronounced dead. Not yet ready for condolences and chatter, I sent out a mass text (so impersonal) at 12:05 a.m. to announce that my daddy had succumbed to his illness. As family and friends started to file into room 332, I sat there in awe. As the room started to thin a little after 3:00 a.m., I sat there for what seemed like hours, just in case he came back, just in case he mumbled something I needed to hear, just in case he had one more last breath. I kept saying, "I can't believe this man is dead." I had never felt so present. Nothing else mattered. I also felt weighted with guilt. Not over what I should have done or told him when he was alive but how things escalated so quickly, and we just stood by...watching. But I couldn't let those types of thoughts inundate my mind. I had just lost my dad, and there was no way I would battle with the family I had left.

My daddy departed this world surrounded by his loved ones and admirers in a beige hospital room, where he was just like anyone else who lost their lives that night ... except to those who loved him. He was not just Mr. Ellison or Patient Ellison in room 332; he was Dad, Daddy, Paw, Uncle Sonny, Sonny, Adam, and Mr. Ellison. He wore many hats, and he was many things to many people. Husband, father, granddad, son, brother, uncle, nephew, employee, inspiration, mentor, coach, leader, example, acquaintance, and friend. The kiss I placed upon his cheek and forehead a minute past five that morning was not on the man I once called Dad but on a corpse. I had waited too long to kiss him. His body was hard and cold. Wow! What a difference 19 days make. My brothers and I had witnessed the last breath of the man partially responsible for our first.

When I got to my mom's place that morning, I lay on the couch and waited for the funeral homes to open. I wept for all who loved my dad, I wept for my dad, but selfishly I wept for myself. Life goes on after tragedy. Losing someone who's been in my life since day one was like losing an organ or limb. I was left to maneuver through life without this intricate part of me, still moving, but noticeably different. Forever changed. Rest well, my love.

In the days following my dad's passing, I kept myself numb by staying busy. From 8:00 a.m. the morning of his death to the day I drove Laila back to school a week later, I made funeral arrangements, created the obituary, planned the repast meal, sat with the girls for hours organizing the photos that family members sent us for the DVD to be played during his wake. My brothers took care of shopping for dad's suit and accessories, as well as helping with the color scheme and casket selection. Like me, I could tell they were doing everything possible to stay preoccupied. Their close friends, who were like brothers, were there as well, running errands, checking on us, printing extra obituaries, and helping during the service so we could just, well ... be. Our mom had done so much already, and we wanted her to get some needed rest and gather her thoughts. She kept busy entertaining friends and family members and ensuring to keep everyone abreast of the service time and location.

Through it all, I got my sister Tai back. It was like the previous disagreement seemed so trivial compared to this. From that first phone call about Dad's diagnosis, she was at the hospital checking on him, calling my brothers, and dropping in on my mom. She put her entire life on hold to support us from the initial diagnosis. That is real love, that's real friendship, that is my sister. It is times like those when you realize what and who matters. The more we lose, the more we cling to what is left.

The day of the funeral came so fast. I'd been to my share of funerals but having to bury a parent was so surreal to me. It was easier to focus on the ceremony to ensure things went smoothly, than to be present and say goodbye to my dad. The loss of a loved one, or someone you cross paths with often, leaves a residue that challenges our mortality. It is difficult to comprehend how we go from laughter, fun, dinners, birthdays, and holiday meals to accepting that someone is forever gone. Clinging only to the memories created. I used to think that funerals were a formal way to say good-bye. But, as I've gotten older, I realized that a funeral is just an opportunity for everyone to see the deceased in their physical state before nature takes its course … one last look.

Our family, like others, has had many funerals. Some expected, most by surprise. The late-night phone call, the news broadcast followed by a barrage of calls, or the frantic friend or co-worker desperately trying to reach you to deliver a message. I believe that once we love someone, we are forever connected; when they pass away, a little bit of us also leaves. I have attended my grandparents, aunts, uncles, cousins, a host of friends, ex-boyfriends, and many associates burials. Funerals can be the hardest part of death because you are inundated with other people's emotions; it's difficult to say anything, let alone "goodbye" or "until we meet again" in a room full of cries, screams, hugs, laughter, confusion, sympathy, and questions. Without a doubt, my daddy's death was so unimaginably difficult to come to terms with, I stopped trying.

We, as a family, had signed off on the very treatment that accelerated his demise. Because of this, we could not provide him with a different set of last days. I saw my dad as a champion, a fighter, and a man of strong will and opinions. It was difficult to accept that he would just give up. Maybe his battle was longer than we all knew, he had lost weight since the party, and it is possible he knew something was wrong, if not exactly what. But not getting a clue that he was ready to leave haunts me like the ghost of Christmas past in a Scrooge movie. But I guess my dad's work on this earth was finished. Things left undone; things left unsaid; it did not matter; it was over. Just like that, no more laughter, no more plans, no more work, no more talks, no more coffee, no more sporting events, no more road trips, no more wins, no more losses, no more anything, but memories. We all will see this day for ourselves when the body becomes hard as stone and cold as winter.

Until we meet again.

MOVING DIFFERENTLY

It has been said that it is not how many times you get knocked down but how many times you get back up. It seemed like I spent most of my adult life recovering from something. As my financial life continued to be a thing of embarrassment, I conducted yet another self assessment to see what I could do that would provide fun and income. A business where, if I worked smart and hard enough, I could create a duplicatable, sustainable entity to leave to my family. I did not lose any sleep over it, I mean, I had become almost immune to the stress of robbing Peter to pay Paul, but I remained open to an array of opportunities. After my dad's passing, we started having weekly family conference calls. These calls were meant to stay in touch and provide everyone a chance to state their week, their intentions for the upcoming week, prayer requests, problem-solving, planning vacations, and everything else. One of those calls call focused on generating additional income. Kei talked about the hair business and some random ladies in Houston who seemed to be capitalizing of it. He explained how they started with booths and tables at college events and grew from there. In a nutshell, he sold me on the idea of selling hair extensions. After all, I had been wearing them since the infamous chemical incident of '93 left me no other choice.

Allow me to travel back to 1993 to give insight into the role hair extensions has played in my life. I always had a nice grade of hair; during my pregnancy with Jaimee, my hair had grown longer than ever. There was this one style I contemplated getting, but my healthy hair stylist refused to do it. So, I found someone who would. The style involved me getting my hair dyed platinum blonde. In the past, I relied on Tai's aunt to dye my hair. But on that fateful weekend, Aunt Catherine was unavailable. So, I allowed another friend to color my hair. She did a pretty good job. The next day went as planned; my appointment with the new stylist was a success. My hair turned out just like I wanted it.

Two weeks later, it was time for me to get a relaxer. This time I scheduled my appointment with my healthy stylist. I saw her give me a disapproving look as soon as I sat down. She looked over my color and extensions that were glued into the freshly dyed hair "Okay, so we're doing a touch-up today, right?" I replied, "Yup." and followed her to the wash bowl, as she proceeded with the touch-up process.; My stylist she said she would let the perm lift the tracks (extensions), and then gently remove them. She didn't want my hair to come out if she pulled on the freshly dyed, weakened blonde hair.

She began to apply the perm and work it generously throughout my hair. I laid back in the shampoo bowl as the perm did its job of straightening my roots and lifting the glue that bonded the hair extensions to my scalp. She put a timer near the bowl and walked off to attend to something else. On this Saturday afternoon, the beauty shop was packed to capacity. When she returned a short time later, she checked my scalp and asked if I was experiencing any burning or itching. "No, I'm fine," was my response.

Suddenly she was in a panic. "Oh hell," was her muffled remark.

"What's wrong?" I quickly snapped.

Without saying a word, she ran her fingers through my hair and came out with a handful of it. Initially, I thought it was just the extensions lifting, but it became painfully obvious that my hair was attached and coming out with the extensions. She quickly rinsed the remaining perm out and removed the remaining extensions from my scalp with a skillful and careful hand. Silence had fallen over the shop as I became the spectacle of the moment. Tai rushed to my aid, only to make matters worse; her facial expression and my stylist's frantic movements were getting the best of my curiosity. Onlookers witness firsthand what became known from that point on as "the incident of '93."

When my stylist sat me in her chair, reality hit me like a tsunami hits land. Where there was once hair, there were remnants of what used to be. I was almost bald from the front of my head to the top of my ears. The poor color application and the hair glue were too much for my hair to survive. The time was 3:12 p.m. It would take everything she had learned in school, plus her many years of experience, to make me presentable again. I would emerge from the salon some eleven hours later with minimum evidence of what happened earlier. Feeling a little more confident than I did earlier in the day, my effort to stay positive and believe it would grow back was shattered as soon as I walked into the house; my dad was like, "Now, what the hell did you do to your hair, Fatou?" Wow—I guess we didn't do such a good job hiding the evidence of a disastrous day after all.

But back to the point I was making about the hair business. After that conversation with my Kei, Her Candy Hair Company, *LLC* was born. I got to work creating a logo, website, cards, registering the LLC, and hiring a marketing person. In the beginning, I had a partner of sorts; she claimed extensive knowledge of the vetting and buying process but proved useless and a time waster. So, I researched, attended events, tried to break into different markets, and eventually built a small clientele. At that point in life, it was what I did to keep busy. After losing my dad, I continued adding more on my plate. I worked full-time, ran Her Candy, and self-studied for the GMAT. Both my dad and Viv's death put things into perspective like no other lesson had. Win or lose, I was going for every damn thing I wanted. I had wasted a lot of time on insignificant people and things. Too many unproductive hours that I couldn't get back. It was time to get shit done. This was 2014.

Before my dad passed, Eric got down on one knee and asked me to marry him. This was his second attempt. I declined both. Although I saw him as one of my best friends, there would be NO happily ever after for us as a couple. He was a great listener and was there when I needed him, but a life with an approval seeker was not in the cards for me. Although I declined the proposal, we remained close., I was on the road to learn that if we don't make decisions, life will do it for us. Throughout our eleven-year friendship/relationship, Eric had come up with hair-brained schemes to obtain the things he had. I had to give him credit, he could get things from barber shops in high-end rent districts to Bentleys', Rolls Royce's', Ferraris, and everything in between. He could make some shit happen, but he never could keep the momentum. I had come to respect the slow and steady because of my past failures. Eric was convinced otherwise. The two perspectives couldn't co-habitat.

But the last straw with Eric came the year following my dad's passing. While making wedding plans with my cousin, to marry me, he started seeing a popular radio personality from the *McCoy Hardee Morning* show. Yes, you read right, he was making plans for us to get married. Without my buy-in. Then on top of his planning, he tried to convince me that this relationship with the radio personality, was going to help launch a reality show centered around the two of them and his growing mobile empire. He went as far as to blame the entire idea on Mr. Hardee. That Mr. Hardee suggested that to move forward successfully, he should have a wife. Eric further explained that Mr. Hardee had the perfect person in mind. Enter his co-host, and Eric's new love interest, Ms. Cherry.

Eric worked hard to convince me to go along with this plan. He wanted me to believe that Ms. Cherry was just a way to get the things in life he was entitled to but had been deprived of because of different obstacles in his life. He said the marriage would be a publicity stunt and would last for one or two years before she divorced him. Such as narcissist. He never considered that I may not want to be associated with someone pulling hustles on women who had worked their way to the top just for him to leech off her. I had to tell him that if he wanted to pursue this venture, our relationship as friends would be over. He later recanted his story and said Mr. Hardee had nothing to do with it, and his friend Renee introduced him to Ms. Cherry, and the three of them came up with the marriage and reality show plan. My advice fell on deaf ears, and five months later, on his 50th birthday, Eric married Ms. Cherry in a star-studded wedding captured in *Ebony* magazine. This fool had the nerve to send me an invitation to the wedding, then continued to call and insist that I see this through. As we say in the south, "Bless his heart". I dodged a bullet.

As close as Jaimee was to my dad, she had yet to display anything but support for me, her granny, her uncles, and her sister after his passing. But she was falling apart inside. She dropped out of college, lied about doing so for a year, racked up unpaid bills everywhere, and became increasingly rebellious. With all I had on my plate, it was difficult to recognize that my child was going through emotional hell until everything in her life was a mess. One of the most frustrating things to do as a parent is to go back and re-raise a child after doing it once. I knew something had to be done, but Jaimee became more stubborn and untrustworthy as she got older. It is hard to make plans and agreements with someone just telling you what you want to hear with no intention of following through. This put a strain on our relationship and another block of bullshit for me to place in my mental bag of things to fix. In her life, Jaimee was blessed with many things—looks, talent, intelligence, patience, and ambition—but her lackadaisical attitude about being honest and accountable made things tougher than they needed to be.

Against my advice, she moved out of my place a week after my dad's funeral. I tried to convince her that staying home, finishing school, working on her craft, and saving money would serve her best in the long run. I might as well have been talking to the television because she did not hear a word I said. That had become our thing; I give her advice and she politely gives it back. But some lessons are best learned the hard way, which she discovered only a few months into her lease. There were conflicts with her roommate over everything from bills to boys. But to save face, Jaimee stuck with her sinking ship like the captain on *Titanic*. After that situation ended, she chucked duces to school and work, left Atlanta, and moved to the big apple. Sounds familiar?

At the time of this book, she has been in New York for over four years, acting in commercials, plays, short films, and web shows. She has not received an Academy Award, but she is well on her way to leaving a legendary footprint in the arts. The independent life looks good on her, and after all my worries, it seems as if she was listening all along. I guess it was all about timing.

I am so proud of my girls. Even with the crap I've put them through, they have become great humans. To hell with the statistics about children from single-parent homes, incarceration, and low income. They have stumbled and succumbed to foolishness like everyone else, but it has always been just that…a stumble. Their norm is caring, loving, professional, creative, hardworking, with an emphasize on family and faith, my pride and joy. Until now, no one knew about their internal struggles, dire circumstances, and heartbreaks because they made it look easy. From mental health issues, father abandonment, and adoption, to college graduates, world travelers, and acclaimed actresses. Jaimee and Laila, my loves, I cannot wait until the rest of the world know what I know.

As for me, I continued my path to purpose. I took the GMAT and started applying to graduate school. Unfortunately, I did not get into the two schools I initially applied to. However, my opportunity came three classes into the graduate curriculum I did get into, *although it wasn't my graduate school of choice*. I received an email invitation to attend an open house for one of the schools that rejected me. On the event day, I was fortunate to overhear a conversation between one of the program directors and a potential student. The director was explaining how the potential student could get into the master's program without taking the GMAT. Pretty certain that my GMAT scores were the reason I wasn't accepted into my top schools, I cornered the director to inquire about this alternative way to admissions. I was thrilled to discover that my work experience could play a big part in getting accepted in lieu of the GMAT. "Really!" We exchanged information, and I followed up the next day. To my delight, my previous application was still active in their system since it was less than a year from my initial admission attempt. All I had to do was resubmitted everything with a test waiver an updated resume and pay the application fee. Fingers crossed.

About two weeks later, I was checking my email, and there it was! **From the Robinson College of Business.** *Congratulations on your recent acceptance to the Masters in International Business program at Robinson College of Business-Georgia State University.* I let out a scream that would have cracked crystal, provided I had any. I was elated. The acceptance proved the power of determination. It validated that a "no" today doesn't mean "no" tomorrow. I withdrew from the program I was in and started the necessary pre work for the accelerated 12-month program I would enter in less than three months. The official letter came two days later. Wow! What a difference a year makes. With each accomplishment, the sins of my past became less relevant.

Two thousand and sixteen was a whirlwind. Jaimee had been in New York for over a year, and Laila was graduating from college the following spring with multiple job offers. I managed to work fulltime, juggle relationships, and promote my business, but graduation was the icing on the cake. This time my mom, niece, daughters, and brothers flew into town to see me walk with my Master's in International Business. MIB. Life was perfect! After graduation, we spent three beautiful days in the Tennessee Mountains. I was a woman in repair no more.

It did not stop there. To honor our dad, grandpa, and husband, we started the *Adam Jackson Ellison Scholarship Fund* to award three graduating students from our high school Alma Malta, (University City Senior High School) a scholarship. In 2019, there was a petition to change the name of the street we grew up on to Ellison Ave. Jaimee starred in a series of commercials and received her first SAG role for a web series; she has since co-written, produced, and starred in a made-for-TV series, *Rock Bottom*. Laila is on the executive leadership team for the most successful food chain in the country. My mom is healthy, vibrant, and enjoying life while raising my niece Kelly (Kame's daughter). She has written a book of poetry and is designing her own line of clothes. Kei is still living his best life, with a son in tow. We were thrilled to welcome Kory Adam to the family. Kame is enrolling in school to complete his degree. Joseline is a successful healthcare administrator and author. I have replaced the stigma of victim, teenage mom, and felon with proud mother, Project Management Professional (PMP), Masters in International Business (MIB), Six Sigma Green Belt, Owner/Founder of Her Candy Hair Company, and now Author.

"Now I know in full" Lessons learned. FM Ellis

There are parts of my past that still affect my present. But each day, I work to become the best version of myself. The failures help me make better choices. The tests helped me grow, the anger turned into peace, the breakdowns became breakthroughs, the self-reflection gave me a voice, the incarceration set me free, and the abuse proved my resilience. My bitter soon became sweet. My lemons made lemonade. I leave with you a few of my lessons learned. Pucker up, people.

Best of life to you all!

🍋 Anything worth having is worth waiting for.

🍋 Those things obtained through deception will not end in your favor.

🍋 The good life is in our perception, not that of others.

🍋 People see you the way you see yourself.

🍋 People are remembered for their impact on others.

🍋 If you know better … do better.

🍋 Ask better questions … heed the answers.

The grass is greener on the other side of the fence, because someone has been watering it. Therefore, if you are standing on dirt, you are irresponsible and negligent at best and should get to work.

A LETTER TO MY FAMILY

Mom and Dad, I love you more than the headache I gave you. I apologize for the pain, agony, financial strain, and mental anguish I inflicted upon you. But, no matter how this life turned out, my mistakes were mine. Not yours.

Mom, you made motherhood look easy, although I learned it is the hardest job in the world. Thank you for your patience and praying spirit. Although I have been a prodigal child most of my life, I have found my way back home.

Dad, thank you for making us read and learn about our history. Because of those lessons, I could carry on and believe in myself when giving up would have been easier. Thank you for your passion and pride; it has been my saving grace.

Kei and Kame, you are more than my brothers; you are my friends. I am proud to be your big sis. You both helped stabilize me without judgment and with unconditional love.

Finally, Jaimee and Laila, you have given me purpose and drive. Being your mom has forced me to become a better human. Because of you, the top of Maslow's pyramid = self-actualization is possible for me. It has been one hell of a ride, and I am honored to have taken it with you. Without your love, laughter, and support, I would have remained in a bad place. For that and for all of you, I am eternally grateful.

I love you.

ABOUT THE AUTHOR

FM Ellis is a newcomer to the literary world. Born and raised in University City, a suburb of Saint Louis, Missouri. She debuted her highly anticipated first book, *My Life as A Lemon; The Memoirs of Me,* in February 2020. A Project Manager by day, and creative writer by night, FM is currently collaborating with her youngest daughter for her sophomore book, *12.23.16.* **Coming Soon!**

She resides in Atlanta, GA, and is the proud glam ma to a beautiful baby boy, L.A.W.

Stay updated with FM Ellis appearances, new material, reader engagement, and more.

@fmellis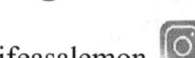

Lifeasalemon

Lifeasalemon.com

<-END->